ST. JOHN PEOPLE

.....a dozen St. John writers profile twenty-two interesting local residents.....

by

American Paradise Publishing, St. John, USVI

This book is dedicated to all the delightfully different peoples of the island of St. John-- especially those who were 'bahn heah' and those who wish they had been.

(ISBN 0-9631060-5-8) First Printing: Sep. 1993
Second Printing: Nov. 1993

 Contact American Paradise Publishing: POB 37, St. John, VI 00831 Telephone (809) 776-8346 or 693-8876 or Answering Service 776-6922.

Special thanks to Keryn Bryan, Robin Miachle, and Kate Norfleet of KATYDIDS for the cover art, and to Lani Clark and Patty McLain for services rendered. Special thanks to artist/photographer Ray Miles for the cover photograph. This project could not have been accomplished without the continuous help of Amy Roberts. American Paradise Publishing would not have come into existence without the long-term support of Cid Hamling and her Connectoids. Thanks!

Table of Contents

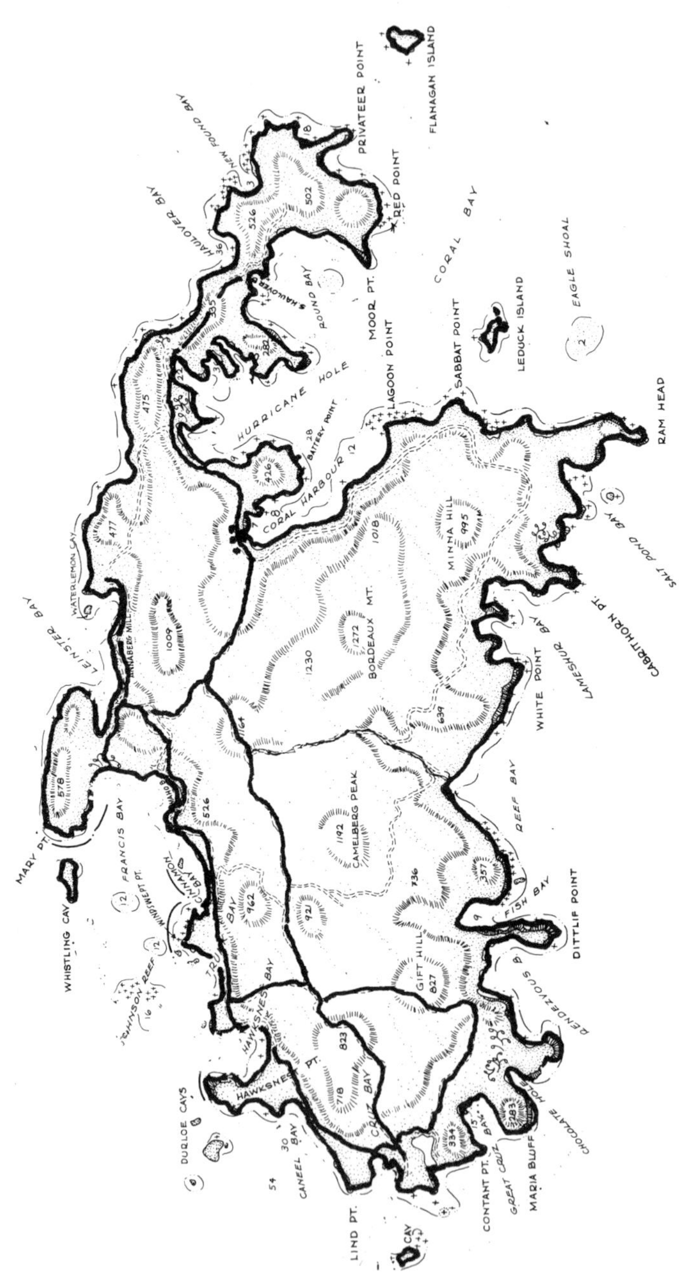

St. John, USVI Latitude 18°20' North Longitude 64°45' West

Introduction

The idea for this book started out as a simple one. I decided to write a book profiling some of the more interesting residents of St. John.

Since I love this island and its people, I believed the project would be an easy one.

However, as soon as I actually began to put pen to paper, I realized how sadly limited the finished product would be if I was the only person involved. No matter how cleverly I might lay the words upon the pages, it would still only be my narrow cultural perspective of my relatively small circle of friends.

One evening after work — as I sipped a cold beer at the Back Yard bar — I thought to myself, "How much better this project would be if a dozen St. John writers were allowed to profile a dozen St. John residents of their own choosing...! How much more rich and diverse and interesting... how much more like St. John itself..."

The rest of the concept immediately fell into place. Instead of writing a book, I decided I'd "skipper" a publishing project focused solely on St. John residents.

My working title was "By, For, and About St. Johnians."

The more I considered the project, the more it excited me. The book would be a reflection of our culture — wildly diverse, genuinely tolerant, mostly loving, and wonderfully chaotic. The readers of the book would not only be able to learn about the people profiled, but also about the writing styles of our local authors. With luck, the resulting book would have an impact far greater than the sum of its parts.

My first concern was whether there were enough skilled writers on St. John to achieve the desired diversity of perspective. Writing is a very sophisticated skill; could this tiny little rock be home to a sufficient number of talented inkslingers?

I grabbed a damp napkin, and scribbled a sloppy list of possible contributors. Yes, it was possible. *If* they would all cooperate.

The idea started to burn within me. It gradually took over my entire professional life. I thought about the project constantly for almost a year — I worried about the tiniest details at the oddest moments. Each evening over dinner my wife Carolyn and daughter Roma Orion would discuss various aspects of it. I became totally convinced that this was a book which needed to be written. That it was a project worth spending a year's worth of my time, talent, and money on. That the result would be something of which all of the people of St. John could be proud of — especially the writers, their subjects, and their families. I wanted to publish a book which would *endure*!

Luckily, I first bounced the idea off Amy Roberts.

Amy is a public school teacher. She is also a writer who frequently contributes to the VI Daily News. She is a long time St. John resident, and loves the island and its people fiercely. I admire her talent and respect her opinion.

She was wildly enthusiastic.

Thus encouraged, I proceeded with confidence.

I'd like to report that the rest was easy, but it was not. In fact, it was anything *but* easy.

I sent out a dozen letters to a dozen writers — and got almost no response. Many were too busy; some didn't trust me or know me or were suspicious of my motives. A number of people turned me down flat, and indicated they thought I would never succeed.

I was flabbergasted by the response — or lack there of.

However, I am not a quitter. It is difficult to discourage me once I have a goal in mind. (It is easy to encourage me; just tell me I can't do something.)

Whenever some aspect of the project would be particularly difficult, I'd call Amy Roberts for solace. She became sort of a de facto co-captain of the project. We'd re-encourage each other; pump ourselves back up.

Some of the stories in this book were only written after I'd called the respective writers numerous times over the course of many months. One or two might only exist because it was easier to actually write the damn piece rather than continue to put up with my constant whining.

It rapidly became apparent to me that the complexity of coordinating a dozen writers — covering twice the number of individual subjects — was an immense task. Each of these stories had to be written, approved by the subject, revised, fact-checked, edited, and proofed. (One subject requested 80 changes in their story!)

Some of the stories required multiple interviews. Some of the authors did extensive pre-interview work, while others did almost none. Three of the stories included were originally written for other publications, and their reprint rights had to be secured. Although I didn't want to have any prior editorial input into the actual stories, all of us involved thought that the final book should be relatively balanced in some subtle and not-so-subtle ways.

Even the easy stuff was hard. The photographs had to be taken, collected, printed, selected, and cropped. That alone took almost a month. Deciding on the illustration for the cover (and its text) took much heated debate.

Frankly, this project required one hell of a lot of groveling & begging & pleading on my part. I wore out my favorite set of knee pads, and my voice became rather hoarse from shouting "please" and "thank you" so often.

Of course, in the end it was all worth it. But I wasn't always sure that it would be as it actually happened.

One of my basic ideas was to allow each of the writers as much artistic freedom as possible. That is what I desired as a professional writer, and thus what I offered as a publisher. I didn't tell my writers who to write about, how to slant their writing, nor did I even hold them to a strict word length. ("Don't leave anything out that should be in, and don't put anything in which should be left out," was as close as I came.)

I told them that we didn't have to worry about producing a particularly scholarly, well balanced overview of contemporary St. John society. (That's a job better left to a professional army of trained historians armed with a handful of NEA grants — not a self-financed commercial publisher such as myself.)

Instead, we should concentrate on allowing some of the love, admiration, understanding, and respect that we have for our fellow island residents to seep out though our pens.

We could shine a sort of literary flashlight into the diversity of our individual lifestyles to modestly illuminate some of the most unique features of our collective society — and thus point out that in some small, important, wonderful ways this island is still a big, sprawling family.

Of course, there are a number of books we *could* have written. We could have written a cute book about charming "old West Indians". Or a funny book featuring the "lush tropical vegetables" which inhabit our rumshops. We could have penned a sea story about our salt-stained "we're-all-here-because-we're-not-all-there!" seafaring community.

Or we could have concentrated on, say, our local "continental" business entrepreneurs, or our indigenous rastafarians, or even the most powerful political group on the island — our taxi drivers.

Instead, we focused on a few almost randomly selected residents. This is not in any-way-shape-or-form a "who's who" of St. John. Any book which doesn't have in-depth profiles of such wonderful people as Miss Elaine, Roy Sewer, Myra Keating Smith and a dozen other local residents certainly can't make that claim. Our basic idea was to take a couple of casual snapshots of ordinary people getting on and off the ferry on any given morning, and circle those individuals we thought might make interesting subjects. One of us came up with a list of 58 people. Another came up with an even longer list, and few overlaps. I'd meet irregularly with various St. John writers at Wendy's (the local "starving artist" hangout), and we'd say, "Yeah, I'll do Mooie. You take Ernest Matthias."

Thus, there are people in this book who probably shouldn't be, and many that should be — but aren't. So be it. If we'd have tried to do it differently, it probably would not have gotten done.

However, we all gradually became convinced that a number of narrowly focused "personality profiles" of local residents written by local residents might better illuminate the colorful social fabric and rich diversity of our society than a broader, more academically aimed brush.

Some of the people within these pages are "bahn here" (born here). Some have resided on St. John for a long time. A few are relatively recent arrivals. Yet all are "St. John People" in the same way New Yorkers are New Yorkers — regardless of where they were born, their race, their religion, their ethnic and cultural roots.

Most of us are here because this island affords us a better quality of life than anywhere else under the American flag. Ask any St. Johnian what he or she would like to change about this island, and they will tell you a hundred different things. And yet most of them couldn't name one single place they'd rather be.

In many ways, contemporary St. John is a state of mind. The majority of its residents were born somewhere else. And many of those who were born here have lived elsewhere.

Thus, St. John is a culture of choice. It has a richly diverse society which has absorbed hundreds of people from every walk of life from all over the globe. For the most part, we all get along remarkably well.

However, St. John society is imperfect. This is clearly reflected in these pages. This island is not a Disney World movie set — nor does it want to be. Every barrel has a few bad apples; ours are both domestic and imported.

But all the people who shared in the writing of this book — and all the people they wrote about — share a fierce love for this island and its people. That's the single common denominator.

Sure, we like to complain and argue and debate and yell at one another sometimes — but most of the people who live on St. John realize that few places on this watery planet afford a better quality of life for such a diverse group of lovable people.

St. Thomas is only a few short minutes away. All of the gaudy glitz of the neon-bejeweled United States of America shimmers just beyond the Cyril E. King airport. The ATM at the Chase bank will be happy to spit out our money; the folks who work at the "At Your Service" travel agency can issue us tickets to anywhere on the planet. All the world honors our American passports.

Yet we cling to this tiny rock. We grow roots. We marry. We raise our families, build our houses, make our homes, argue, dance, laugh, love, and ultimately die here.

Why?

I hope at least some of the answers to these questions are contained within these pages.

Cap'n Fatty Goodlander

An Ultra Brief History of St. John

The Virgin Islands are located 1493 miles south of Cape Sable, Nova Scotia, 1,100 miles southeast of Miami, and just 14 miles east of Culebra, Puerto Rico. Christopher Columbus "discovered" them on his second voyage in 1493-- over a thousand years after they'd been settled by the peaceful Arawak Indians, who, at that point in time, had been driven out by the more war-like Caribs.

The Virgin Islands were soon invaded by the French, English, Spanish, Danes, and Dutch — with the Danes firmly in control of St. John and St. Thomas by 1666. The governing Danish West Indian Company (an early multinational corporation) encouraged local planters to produce sugar cane. To accomplish this, they imported slaves from Africa, mostly from Ghana.

In 1733 Denmark bought St. Croix from the French, and the three main islands remained under Danish rule until March 31, 1917 when they were sold to the United States of America for $25,000,000, which was about $300 an acre.

Although the 27,000 slaves in the Territory were technically "freed" in 1848, they were, in reality, kept under such tight legal, social, and economic restraint that their new-found "freedom" was more illusionary than real.

On St. John, there was a successful island-wide slave upraising in 1733. Participants were able to hold the island for almost six months before being recaptured by the combined forces of the Danish and French militias. At the height of the plantation period, St. John had a slave population of nearly 2,000. With the decline of agricultural profits in the late 1800's, most of the plantations ceased operations. The residents of St. John were then left to their own devices. The population bottomed out at around 700 as St. John quietly slipped back into obscurity.

In the early 1950's another power shift took place — Laurance Rockefeller purchased large tracts of St. John and donated them to the (1956) National Park Service.

Today the island of St. John (21 square miles, about the same size as Manhattan) is two-thirds National Park, and has a steady year-round population of about 3,500 people. Over a million tourists visit annually.

MOOIE

by
Amy
Roberts

When you step off the ferry on St. John on a typical afternoon, you're immediately caught in a swirl — of students in pink and maroon uniforms streaming off the school boat — of tourists in skimpy neon playsuits roaming in a rum-and-sun-dazed haze — of taxi drivers hustling up work– of Jeeps crowding the curb — of T-shirts clamoring to be bought.

Cruz Bay is not the sweet, sleepy little town it was 50, 20 or even 10 years ago. Bustling, commercial, and even self-consciously cute, Cruz Bay has become a hopping, "happ'nin" little place.

But maybe, as you step off the ferry, you're looking for something else — something of the old St. John, something more authentically West Indian. Look around. There is one spot left. You might miss it, although it's right around the corner and painted an eye-catching shade of pink. It's Mooie's Bar.

"The place hasn't changed since I opened it — on December 23, 1956," said Mooie. "The prices don't change. I don't carry no fancy drinks. The guys go in and shoot the breeze. The only thing that's changed is the counter; it used to be a horseshoe."

Actually, one other thing has changed. For years when Mooie served as St. John's senator on St. Thomas, he would leave the bar unattended. "I couldn't afford to pay anyone to work, so I left it open and people would serve themselves. I didn't have a cash register — people would leave the money on the shelf." The only thing that was ever stolen, he added, was one coin out of a framed collection mounted on a wall.

Those trust-based days are gone, but Mooie's remains one of the last traditional rum shops on the island. It is frequented almost exclusively by locals (although a few tourists, lured by the sign rightly proclaiming "The coldest beer in town," do venture in.)

The decor is simple — assorted chairs, formica tables, fluorescent lights, a fan, blue wooden walls hung with a few signs, and a stack of trophies. You won't find ferns, or frothy blender drinks, or video games. If you're not a regular customer, the guys hanging around Mooie's will check you out as you come in; if you're female, they'll check you inside-out.

Mooie's is owned by Theovald E. Moorehead — a.k.a. "Mooie." The small, handpainted wooden signs on the building are the only indication to passers-by that the Moorehead family owned — and still controls — much of the property in the heart of Cruz Bay.

In fact, most of the private property adjoining Cruz Bay Park was the Moorehead family's yard. (That's how the Backyard Bar got its name, in case you've ever wondered.) If you know what to look for, you'll see other clues of the family's dominion. Miss Meada's Shopping Mali is named for Mooie's half-sister, who used to have a restaurant at the site (as did her mother before her.) Miss Meada's twin, Miss Myrah Keating Smith (the midwife for whom the St. John's clinic is named) still lives in the house above Stitches, where the old family home was located. (The original wooden frame house was replaced by the existing two-story block structure in the 1980's). And though people may call the edifice across from Chase Bank "the Connections Building," it is officially titled the Theo Moorehead Building.

Although he lives upstairs, you probably won't see Mooie hanging out in his bar. He rarely takes a drink now, and besides, he's got other things to do. If you need something notarized, you might meet him. Sturge, the bartender for the last 20 years, will direct you through a maze of cartons in the bar's storeroom to Mooie's office in the back.

There you'll see him — a very tall, erect man in his seventies, with chiseled cheek bones and sharp eyes that take in everything from behind thick glasses. His manner is polite, businesslike, his voice is husky and low. But he can change in a matter of seconds, warming to an old friend who drops by for a favor, or raging at a ditzy tourist who thoughtlessly parks in his yard.

"Positive, stubborn, bullheaded — and kind," is how Mooie describes himself. But to some, he brings to mind the image of a mahogany tree — coppery-colored, tall, strong, resistant, and staunchly West Indian.

Although he prefers to keep a low profile these days, Mooie continues to be an important figure on St. John. His business enterprises have included real estate management and appraisals, construction and development. He served as senator in the Legislature for 16 years. He was one of the founders of St. John's first ferry company, and he still holds the concession to develop the boat yard in Coral Bay.

Over the years he's been involved with a dozen civic organizations and government agencies, including the Lions Club, the Boy Scouts, the Small Business Administration, the Port Authority, the Insurance Commission, and the Lutheran Church.

But Mooie made his reputation as a passionate defender of the rights of native property owners. To this day, he remains a fierce critic of the federal government's takeover of the island through the creation of the Virgin Islands National Park.

Mooie was born in 1916, the youngest child of police officer Edward Alfred Moorehead and Eugene Theodora Keating. Edward was one of three brothers whose family emigrated from Sint Maarten. The brothers dispersed, each one settling on (what are now) the three U.S. Virgin Islands. Thus, despite spelling variations, most of the Mooreheads throughout the territory are related.

This was not the only generation of Mooreheads to migrate in search of a better life. "There was a period in these islands when it was tough to make a living," explained Mooie, recalling his early childhood. "Many went to the Dominican Republic; it was the easiest place to get work." His two eldest half-brothers, Roderick, a teacher on St. Thomas, and Euclid, a fisherman, left in search of a better life, and the family never heard from them again.

St. Johnians in those days made their living by fishing and farming, supplying St. Thomas with fruits and vegetables for food, and charcoal and wood for fuel. "It was the barter system back then. If I had potatoes and you had yams, we'd swap," said Mooie.

The Mooreheads had a huge garden brimming with "cassava, potatoes, pigeon peas — you name it. On Saturday, every kid from the whole community would come here to play," Mooie recalled. But before the fun could begin, there were chores to complete. The garden had to be "weedless." The household silver needed to be polished by hand with a fine powder pounded from red brick. The Mooreheads also had cattle and horses up in the hills. "One of the things we had to do was oil the harness and wax the saddles — they had to glisten, they had to shine! We'd do what Tom Sawyer did — get the other kids to help and get it done in a few minutes," Mooie smiled.

Mooie attended the Bethany School (now the parish meeting room at the Bethany Moravian Church) until sixth grade. St. Johnians who wanted further education had to go off island, and Mooie was one of the lucky ones whose family could afford to send him to school on St. Thomas. While a student at Charlotte Amalie High School, he boarded with a family and came home only on weekends. "Your parents sacrificed to send you to school," he said fiercely. "You *had* to learn. You couldn't go back and tell them you failed. They'd kill you!"

Mooie calls modern education in the Virgin Islands "a disgrace!"

"They're turning out illiterate kids in the 12th grade," he complained. "How many people do you see now with a newspaper? People don't read. We didn't have newspapers — they were an expensive thing in those days. The teacher had one, and everybody learned from it."

He wants to revamp the education system by giving authority back to the classroom teacher, like in the old days. "You respected the teachers tremendously [back them], and you liked them. The teacher would slap you around, and then they'd tell your parents about it, and then you'd be damned sorry because you'd get another beating, too!"

But despite the problems, teachers in those days taught the children well. He recalls one educator, Ann Benjamin, who wisely tossed out the textbook when things didn't apply to the Virgin Islands. "There was this mathematical problem about a train going from New York to California. She said to the class, 'Forget this! Have you been to New York? We're going to talk about a jackass going from Cruz Bay to Coral Bay!'"

After graduating in 1936, Mooie returned to St. John and became the island's first Immigration and Customs Inspector. It was through this job that he met his wife, the former Genevieve Hendricks. His position required him to make weekly trips to Coral Bay (which then had a larger population than Cruz Bay) to collect customs reports. There he met his wife-to-be at a party, but they didn't marry until seven years later.

Mooie attributes the long courtship to two causes: first, "Marriage was a helluva responsibility in those days," he explained, and second, "When you met a girl, it was a problem. You didn't have a moment alone with her! She was always with her mother, or the minister's wife, or with Miss Gerda Marsh, who had activities for girls." The young men had a chance to mix with the young ladies of the island at cricket matches, where the males (batting left handed as a handicap) took on the females.

Mooie was kept plenty busy as Immigration and Customs Inspector. There was a lot of smuggling back then, especially of Tortola-made cane rum. Mooie routinely uncovered demijohns of rum listed on the customs documents as ballast.

Livestock were another common form of contraband. Red Hook didn't exist as a port, so St. Johnians and Tortolans had to sail (or row their boats on windless days) all the way to Charlotte Amalie. Many a cow died in transit, so smugglers would try to swim them ashore at Red Hook.

The import duty back then was 25 cents, which Mooie termed "a helluva lot of money" back when laborers made less than 60 cents a day. So Mooie used his discretion when giving out fines. "They weren't trying to commit a crime; they were trying to make a living. I'd give them a warning; sometimes I'd confiscate [the contraband] but I wouldn't put it in a report."

Since Mooie also served as clerk of the court (and his father was the sole police officer), he was familiar with all the crime on St. John. "The highest fine ever levied was $3 — for slander," Mooie reported. Slander was the island's most common crime in those days, although once in a while, somebody would steal something "for use" — a goat, or a machete.

There was one violent murder, however, back in around 1938. Miss Anna Marsh, a woman in her 50's, lived alone in Reef Bay. Hearing a suspicious sound, she went outside armed with a shotgun to investigate and was attacked by a robber hiding in her guava tree. He killed her with her own gun.

The murderer was traced after someone recognized a brooch (worn by a woman on St. Thomas) as a piece of jewelry stolen from Miss Marsh. The killer was caught and sentenced to life in prison. In this small-island world where justice was likely to prevail, crime simply didn't pay.

Mooie can only shake his head at the extent of crime on St. John now. He blames it on "the influx of dope," which is caused by a combination of an ailing economy and the deterioration of the family on St. John. "If we had an economy which was bright, we'd have a good school system, and we'd have a wife staying home. Now when a child leaves the home for school, he's alone. He comes back to an empty house, so he remains on the street. There's no contact between parent and child, not because they don't love them, but because parents are too damned tired when they reach home," he railed.

Mooie did his share to help the youths of St. John in his day. As an intrepid Boy Scout leader, he'd take the likes of Llewellyn Sewer, Julian Harley and Noel Boynes on wilderness camping adventures to Little Cinnamon and Francis bays. The scouts would carry no supplies and exist exclusively on what they could catch. "If you can't find something, you'll starve!' I'd tell them." They became experts at crabbing and fishing, he remarked, slightly smiling at the recollection.

"But that was before the park had taken over lock, stock, and barrel, telling you what to do and where you could go," he added pointedly. Mooie's attitude changes quickly when he gets on the subject of the National Park. Don't try to tell him how beautiful it is, or how it's one of the territory's strongest attractions, or how the Park Service protects the land. "Protect from what?" he'll counter. "Our forefathers protected it for centuries. The park isn't protecting any natives!"

"Their attitude is a frightening thing," he continues. "'Don't make them slaves as they used to do; instead, make them economic slaves.'" Mooie believes that the park's acquisition of natives' land has robbed the former landowners of their economic freedom, and ultimately their autonomy. "When you've got the 'green stuff' in your hand, or in the bank, that's freedom. People here will never be free," he said, shaking his head.

His battle with the National Park began in 1955. Mooie was in the Army then, stationed in France, when he saw a copy of *The Saturday Evening Post* with a picture of Senator Julius Sprauve shaking hands with Laurance Rockefeller. An accompanying article proclaimed the upcoming dedication of the Virgin Islands National Park.

Mooie was outraged. He marched into his superior's office the next day with his request for discharge, prematurely ending his military career. Seventeen days later he was out.

"I came home selfish, to protect the piece of land I had, not to save the island," Mooie said matter-of-factly. Then he became agitated. "Do you know what they planned to do? They planned to condemn the entire island! That's something you don't hear much of anymore. The idea was to move everybody on the island to Green Valley [Fish Bay] and the Battery was going to be the Park Headquarters. They never talk about this thing now!"

Mooie spent 10 days in Washington "lobbying like hell" — collaring senators and congressmen, and placing ads in the Washington *Post* to inform the public of the plan to take over the island. His efforts paid off and the amendment which mandated the condemnation was defeated. Mooie became a local hero. He also developed a reputation in the Capital. "Washington has a dossier on me as thick as your arm," he says proudly.

Actually, the dossier probably dates back to 1944 when Mooie's "subversive" activities began. Like many Virgin Islanders then, he was working for the Navy on St. Thomas as a civilian clerk. America was at war, and Mooie seriously considered enlisting in the Navy. "But you see, because of my color, I was going to have to change rank. I would have had to have been a mess steward, so I said, 'To Hell with that!'"

The military was strictly segregated then, and blacks were excluded from combat. Ironically, several months later, Mooie was drafted by the Army. He was one of 540 Virgin Islanders who were drafted or enlisted. The Virgin Islanders, however, proved to be a problem for the racially segregated Army. "They didn't know what the hell to do with us!" Mooie recounted. "They had two types of Puerto Ricans, the black ones they called 'madama' and the ones that were supposed to be white, or 'clear.' But we didn't fit in anywhere, so they had to form a battalion for us." After receiving basic training, they were sent to a base near New Orleans.

In retrospect, the Army would no doubt say it made a mistake by keeping the Virgin Islanders together. When the men arrived in the South and experienced the effects of racial segregation for the first time in their lives, they took it as a joke. Then they got mad.

"They used to have some signs at the back of the bus — 'Colored patrons only' — we took the damn signs down and threw them out! The bus drivers told the other passengers, 'Sit down — these people ain' from here; they're from Puerto Rico or some other damned place.'"

On their days off, Virgin Islanders would band together and leave camp deliberately planning to create some kind of disturbance, according to Mooie. "Canal Street in those days was the widest street. It was the first place we saw neon lights, but you wouldn't see a colored person on the whole damned street. We'd go down 14 strong, walking abreast, and take up the whole street. Instead of colored people walking off the sidewalk [to get out of the way of white people], white people had to get out of the way for us!

"We had a guy in the outfit — an engineer — who was a solid Catholic. He peeped into the church and saw only white people, so he was scared to go in. So seven of us went in and started to go up the aisle. A guy touched us and said, 'Colored can't go down there!' I said, 'What you telling me?' and we went up the aisle." But the engineer ultimately decided to attend the Baptist Church on a regular basis. "We knew it could become a violent thing, and you couldn't fight in church."

Ironically, the majority of black soldiers on the base, who were mostly from the South, did not support the Virgin Islanders' actions. "We found ourselves physically fighting them all the time," said Mooie. "When we had a company party, we'd tell them not to come because they were so different from us. It was like chalk was to cheese. They said we were white because of our attitude! It was a bigger segregation situation between us and them than between us and the white soldiers."

Eventually, the Virgin Island soldiers decided to take action directly against the military in an event that became known as the Camp Plauche Affair. "They had a separate PX for black soldiers. The club had a nickelodeon and a pool table, and that was it. We had to ask for a Coke machine. Then we decided, 'The hell with it! We're going in to the main PX!'"

"We created a riot. They put gas around us, disarmed us, and cordoned us off with military police and other soldiers so we couldn't leave the barracks. Then they hurried up and shipped us out to the West Coast."

Mooie and his cohorts were eventually sent to Hawaii to work as stevedores. (The Army figured that since they were from the islands, they were familiar with ships.) "We were at Sand Island, right below Diamond Head. Everything for the Pacific came in there, we worked day and night," he said.

When the war was over, Mooie, who had a wife and only one dependent daughter, didn't qualify for immediate discharge. After staying on for several months, he decided to make the military his career. During his 12 years with the Army, he served in locations throughout Europe, the U.S., and the Caribbean. "Governor Farrelly, and Governor King were in my outfit," Mooie said. "I used to tell them I'm a 30 year man. That was until the National Park caused me to get out."

In 1956, Senator Julius Sprauve decided to retire and urged Mooie to run in his place. His opponent was "Duke" Ellington, a white statesider who owned the land near Gallows Point (for whom the resort's restaurant is now named.) Mooie won.

Once again, Mooie decided to go into battle, this time in the political arena. With the help of Rafael "Lito" Valls from St.

Croix, Ron deLugo and others, Mooie began organizing the Democratic Party to challenge Earle Ottley's Unity Party, which dominated the Senate. "The Unity Party was a political machine, like Tammany Hall. Ottley was, and is, a master politician. He's got politics down to a science. He is a guy who is very dedicated to what he is doing," said Mooie, with a mixture of contentiousness and admiration.

"As president of the Legislature, Ottley was the only guy to have a chauffeur. (The rest of us had only one car.) But his chauffeurs wouldn't last! He'd burn them out! He would have them come pick him up at 4:00 a.m. because someone would call and say his step was broken, and he'd go to show them he was there. Earle Ottley looked out for you. I couldn't join him because he had control. I couldn't live with that."

In all, Mooie spent 16 years in the Senate, traveling to St. Thomas during the week and returning to St. John on weekends, as in his high school days. For six months of work, two weeks in session and two weeks off, senators earned an annual salary of $600 — less than a one-hundredth of what they make now. "No businessman would run for the Senate," he claimed. "You had to be somebody with money; only they could afford [to serve]." These days Mooie generally views politics with disgust. "The people in charge — they don't give a damn. They're only collecting a salary. There's no dedication to what they've got to do... It seems to me St. John was always...more," he said, his voice trailing off.

A career in politics eventually proved to be too exhausting — spiritually and financially. When Mooie left the Legislature in 1971, he went into the construction business full time, building houses for people on contract. "I had to make some kind of living," he explained. "The way to make money was to make speed and get out. You can't save on material, but you can save on labor," he said.

Mooie's father had taught him carpentry, along with other valuable skills, while he was growing up. ("My father believed that he could do everything, and he taught us everything. He was an unusual man," he said shaking his head in admiration. "He was something else.")

Mooie rates the restoration of the Enighed Great House (now the island's museum and library) as one of his greatest accomplishments. But one thing about that job that broke his heart was the government's decision to paint the interior white. "The whole of the inner paneling is mahogany, and nobody would know! It's a disgrace!" he said throwing up his hands. Mooie was so upset about the decision that he contacted Governor Cyril King to pressure him to halt the paint job. But his efforts came too late.

Another of Mooie's business ventures was the first scheduled ferry service to St. Thomas. "I found when I came home from the military that there was no transportation here. One day I was shooting the breeze in the bar with Victor Sewer, and [Ron] Morrisette [Sr.], talking 'bout this thing and we said, 'Why the hell we don't form a company and buy a boat?'" They formed the St. John Corporation to run ferries from Cruz Bay to Red Hook, a 40 minute trip. Their first boat was *The St. John*. Soon they added two more to their fleet — *The Grey Gull*, and *The Explorer*. Mooie was vice-president of the company for eight years, until 1958, when he clashed with the board of directors and quit.

The marine industry has always appealed to Mooie, although, it hasn't necessarily led to success. As a senator, he introduced the legislation to build the yet-to-be developed marina at Enighed Pond. Since 1979, he's been president of the St. John Boat Yard, the company which holds the lease to develop a marina in Coral Bay. "It's had all kinds of problems," he said with agitation, referring to the latter project. "Four different times we've had financing in place, and lost it because of the dragging feet of the Port Authority, or the Department of Planning and Natural Resources. And Coral Bay needs something to stimulate the economy! It's like Frederiksted. They're the two most economically depressed areas in the Virgin Islands. The tourist dollars don't reach over there."

Mooie says the government has thwarted his plans to develop his property in Cruz Bay as well. At one point he intended to expand the building that now houses the bar, but "With all the parking spaces I'd have to build there, I'd be left with a building you could span with your hand. So I said, 'I don't need it.'"

Cultural conservationists will be pleased to know that Mooie's

Bar is in no immediate danger of disappearing. Mooie plans to hold on to the property and predicts that his daughter (Theodora Moorehead, who lives in New York) will sell it "when she gets disgusted with St. John. I've reached that stage where I get so disappointed so often!"

Mooie admits to a certain level of pessimism regarding St. John's future. "I don't have much hope for St. John, and do you want to know why? Hope is in the hands of the coming generation," he stated. "And unless you have an educated generation, you ain' going no place! This generation doesn't know what's going down. They're centered around a TV, a car, a gold chain — the tangible things."

The blame for the current state of affairs must be shared, Mooie believes. Laurance Rockefeller and the federal government are responsible for taking the land from the natives to establish the park. But also to blame are "the generation of St. Johnians that is willing to sell a piece of land for a Cadillac. Those who have no investment in the island have no stake in seeing it improve," Mooie contends.

"Unless you own a piece of St. John, it doesn't mean a thing to you. But if you own a piece, it will draw you back," he says, bringing to mind the image of the mahogany tree again. "It's only because of the roots I stay."

Amy Roberts moved to St. John in 1983. She teaches English at the Ivanna Eudora Kean High School on St. Thomas, and regularly writes for the VI Daily News and other publications.

HERMAN PRINCE

by
Dana Harrison

He was born in 1913, the first child of John and Helen Prince, born in the same house that his mother was born, on the same spot in Zootenval that his house now stands. Zootenval was a sleepy settlement then as it is now, tucked deep in the heart of Coral Bay with the East End stretching beyond it. A few hip roofed houses dotted the hillsides surrounded by cattle pasture. There were no cars, phones, radios or electricity. There weren't even ice cubes for the limeade. But there were donkeys to ride, boats to row, and candles to light. There were neighbors to share with and to spread their small news — neighbors who were family, even if they weren't. Life was hard and always on manual, yet life was good. "How was it good?" I asked. "People seemed happier then," he told me. And his smile told me so.

When I asked Herman about his life, he told me about his children. There is Ralph, Kenneth, Bert, Risza, and Ann. All of his children are living fruitful lives, and all except Bert still live in the Virgins. After telling me about his children, Herman began telling me about his 15 grandchildren. Soon I had to stop him "Could you tell me about you?" I reminded him. There is no doubt that family ranks high on his list of values; I could tell this from his eyes, as well as the words he spoke.

When Herman was eight, he moved from his grandmother's house in Zootenval up to Johnny Horn where his parents and four sisters lived. Johnny Horn was an old village that hid over the hill between Emmaus and Leinster Bay. Only a few families lived there; the houses were surrounded by cultivated land and cattle pastures.

From his window, Herman saw Tortola with Drake's Channel between their shores. Tall ships and other sailboats would sometimes pass, adding detail to the panorama of blues and greens.

Leinster Bay was a walk around the point, and it was there where his father's fishing boat would rest, and there where the children would sometimes go to swim. Herman was a tall, lanky boy then who was active and hard-working. Though there was time to relax, there were also a lot of chores to get done. He would make fishtraps for his father, baskets for his mother and tend to the cattle, fruit trees, gardens, and fences that spread out over the hills.

Coral Bay was a barefoot half hour walk to the south. The trail would lead up passed the gut and mission's horse fields, up the hill behind the Moravian Church. From there he could view both sides of his world. Behind him to the north lay Johnny Horn with the British Islands in the distance, and in front of him lay Coral Bay with the East End stretching out in a dwindling string of mountains and bays. The Carolina valley was cleared pastureland and the bay was calm and clear except for the dark blotches of jack fish and the few small row boats pulled up along its shore. The world seemed so grand to Herman when he was nine looking down from the top.

The church was also down below him with its red roof and open doors. He would spend his Sunday mornings at the church from then until this day, and his school days were spent at the school that sat close beside it.

Benjamin Franklin School as it was then called, was a two room school house which went up to the 6th grade. There were two teachers then and a traveling principal who oversaw the three small schools scattered about the East End. Mr. Ernest Sewer, the basketry teacher, would also come to the school in the afternoons to teach the children basket-making with hoop vine.

Basketry required a lot of patience, skill, and determination for a child or an adult to master. The vine had to be cut just before the new moon, then split, stripped and woven into the baskets. Fish traps could be woven as well as the round and ribbed baskets. The ribbed "market" baskets soon became the most popular of the hoop products and the East Enders of St. John became the masters of their work. The baskets became standard utility baskets and were used for carrying produce to and from the market as well as for carrying anything from bread to babies.

The Moravian missionaries who sailed over from Europe in the 1700's are believed to have been the first teachers of the market basket construction. They adapted the ribbed baskets, made of oak and hickory in their homeland, to incorporate the use of the local hoop vine, a sturdy vine that was plentiful and easy to work with. The missionaries passed on their craft, as well as their religion, and soon the East End of St. John was busy exporting the baskets to St. Thomas and other far off shores. Herman perfected the craft as well, but it wasn't until later in life when his basket skills were really put to use.

"It is very important to make an honest living in life," he would tell me. There was no government aid to fall back on, no unemployment or welfare funds. People had to work and provide for themselves and their family. And when school ended for Herman after 6th grade, work began. He became an apprentice to Harry Samuel at 15 and began work learning masonry. His first major project as an apprentice was adding the second building to the Benjamin Franklin school that had schooled him. After that, many jobs followed and they eventually led him to Caneel Bay where he worked as a mason and laborer for nine years.

Caneel at this time was in the beginning stages of resorthood.

It was owned by the Danish West Indian Company and consisted of seven cottages for the new breed of "tourists" and three long barracks where the workers slept. During the week, Herman would stay there as well, but on weekends he was quick to ride his horse over the hillsides that led back to Johnny Horn.

Maybe those long weeks away from home got him thinking about family. And it wasn't long before Euphema Thomas caught his eye and his heart. She was a cook at Caneel and stayed there for most of her days off since her home in St. Thomas was too far for weekly travel. They fell in love and walked down the aisle in February, 1943. After their marriage, the Princes moved to Zootenval, back to where Herman was born. Their first baby was born nine months later.

In the 1940's things slowed at Caneel because of the war. It was then that his basket skills proved a viable asset. Senator Julius E. Sprauve approached him about teaching basketry in the schools and Mr. Prince soon agreed. In 1946, he began his work as basket teacher to the children of St. John. There were four schools at the time, in East End, John's Folly, Coral Bay and Bethany (which moved down to Cruz Bay a few years later). He visited one school each day of the week, with an extra day spent at Benjamin Franklin School. He would arise early in the morning and ride out to the school of the day with his hoop vine strapped to his side.

He enjoyed his job as basket teacher and became known throughout the island for his work. His earlier years as a public school teacher were his best. He taught all the students then, and he relished in the diligence and the courtesy and respect they showed for him and for each other. As the school population steadily grew, problems grew along with it. Soon he was forced in school to limit his talents to the slower learners. After thirty years of teaching basketry in the public schools, he retired from his post, hoping that some of the skills he taught would still be passed on.

Herman didn't give up on teaching entirely after he retired. He continued to give adult classes through the National Park. On Wednesday afternoons you could see him down at Hawksnest Beach surrounded by women and baskets.

When I asked previous students to tell me about Mr. Prince as a teacher, I was greeted with moments of silence. How could they describe this teacher, who taught them more about life than just basketry? Words were hard to come by. "He is a natural born teacher who really enjoyed his work," one student told me. "He's a real story teller," said another. "He came off as being strict and would chastise me for talking too much, or coming to class late, or having dull rib points, but he said it all with a sparkle in his eyes and I knew he was only teasing." Another student summed it up in just a short line, "Well, of course, we think the world of Mr. Prince." And it seems like everyone who knows him feels the same way.

Although Herman's teaching days are now over, he still weaves baskets with hands that remain strong and nimble. His baskets have become small treasures of a fading past. He still lives in Zootenval in his bright yellow cottage surrounded by a garden in bloom. His wife, Euphema, is still there by his side. The old community of Johnny Horn, where Herman spent much of his childhood, is now in ruins as the people who once lived there either died with the years or were forced to move closer to the main stream of progress.

"You have to earn a living and pay your way in life," he told me once again. Maybe life isn't a free gift to use up, but a gift to add to and pass on. I watch his hands weaving the "God's Eye" into his next basket, the diamond anchoring handle to frame. I catch the sparkle in his eye, and take it with me as I go.

Dana Harrison was born in New York. She has Master's Degree in Education from UVI. She currently serves as the Elementary Guidance Counselor for both St. John schools. Her craft book 'Of Hands and Earth' was published in 1992.

Peter Muilenburg

by

Cap'n Fatty Goodlander

"There were times when I was scared, real scared," said Peter Muilenburg. "The Deep South was, at least for me, a dark and violent place 30 years ago — all those swampy, moss-covered magnolia trees in Alabama seemed evil. A lot of people in the movement died — mostly black Mississippians. I'd been shot at, beat up, arrested, held in solitary confinement — even hit with a cattle prod. Sometimes I wondered just what the hell I thought I was doing."

"The worst time was in Natchez, Mississippi. We'd organized a large civil rights demonstration, during which I'd been arrested. Racial tensions were running high. When they were putting me in jail, I asked to be put in with the blacks — my friends. I felt I'd be safer there. But because I was white, they refused. I thought, 'This is it! I'm going to be beaten, maybe killed...', but to my surprise the white inmates didn't bother with me. They were a little scornful, but after awhile there was no problem."

"However, the jailer hated me. He was an old guy, and being a jailer was his part-time job. He lived in the back of the same building the jail was in. He must have been about 70, and he would stand outside my cell, grab the bars, rattle them with rage, and start vilifying me. 'You nigger loving son of a bitch!' he'd scream. He'd work himself into such a fit that foam would flick from the corners of his mouth..."

"One night there was a rustling outside the window of my cell. Something or someone was moving in the bushes. I froze; listened — there it was again! I was convinced it was a gunman. I was sure I was going to be shot. So I did the best I could to protect myself. There was a steel girder in my cell, and I discovered I could hide almost half my body behind it. I could either protect my body from head-to-waist or below my belt. It wasn't fun attempting to decide which parts I valued more! Frankly, I didn't want to lose *anything..!* As it turned out, it was probably just a stray dog taking a piss against the wall or something — but for me it was a long night."

Being a 'Freedom Rider' in the American civil rights movement back in the 1960s required a tremendous commitment to The Cause — and not a small measure of personal courage. Peter Muilenburg had — and has — plenty of both.

However, Peter is uncomfortable with being cast in even a slightly heroic light. He insists his role was a minor one. "Sure, I was committed to helping all Americans gain their full civil rights — but it was also an adventure. It wasn't all idealism on my part. In many ways it was fun. I came-of-age during that time — became a man. I learned a lot. There was a tremendous comradery within the movement. We lived on almost nothing. That's how I acquired my taste for hot sauce..."

Peter and his friends in the movement often stayed in dilapidated 'Freedom Houses' along the way. Sharing their food was mandatory. But Peter quickly discovered that by doctoring his rice and beans with a massive amount of hot/hot/hot sauce — not too many people wanted to share his meal.

"Nobody had any money. People were always passing through. It was only good manners to share what you had. But often, there just wasn't enough food to go around. So I soon got hip to the hot sauce trick. That's one of the reasons I love the West Indies so much — every where you go, there's a new hot sauce to taste!"

Peter Muilenburg was born in New York in 1945. At the time, his missionary father (John P.) was attending Cornell University, studying the Chinese language. Within the year, the family was in China — just in time for the revolution.

"The Communists hadn't taken over yet when we first got there. They were up in the north, gathering their strength, and gradually making their way south to where we were. But Chiang Kai-shek's Nationalist government was already crumbling. It was obvious that it was going to fall because it was so corrupt and didn't offer much for the people."

The fighting got closer and closer. Peter's earliest memories center around the mammoth conflict.

"One morning I was putting syrup on my pancakes," Peter said, "when we suddenly heard a plane. Usually, we could hear a plane coming a long way off, but this one was different. It was right there overhead and the bombs were coming down and the house was shaking and — whack! — the ceiling plaster fell down right onto my pancakes. I can still remember that as clear as if it was yesterday. It was terrifying, and yet sort of funny too."

"I can also recall distinctly our bomb shelter — how the pick axe marks looked in the hard-packed earthen floor near the door, and its bracing of the heavy wood — and how cool, nice, and safe it felt within."

"My father could see that the government of Chiang Kai-shek wasn't acting in the best interests of the people — and he was somewhat sympathetic to the reformers. So when the Communists finally came to power, he was one of the few missionaries who were invited to stick around. I'm not attempting to make him out to be a Fellow Traveler or anything, but very few of the other missionaries were allowed to stay."

The Communists took over in 1948, and within two years it was readily apparent to Peter's father that a person with deep religious convictions wasn't going to be happy in China.

"We had to smuggle ourselves out of China because the Nationalists were blockading the harbor," Peter recalls. "We waited a number of tense days for a cloudy, stormy, moonless evening — and were taken aboard a funky old British tramp streamer. If the Nationalists had spotted us, we'd have been sunk on sight. I was five years old at the time, and I can distinctly remember feeling the salty sea breeze on my face and the warm sunshine the next morning — we were finally clear of China."

The Muilenburg family then moved to the Philippines. "Father wasn't your stereo-typical bible-thumping missionary. He was more a helper and teacher with a strong Christian faith. I guess, in a way, he too was looking for adventure — that he too was living his dream."

Even as a youngster, Peter loved books — especially biographies and historical novels. Perhaps growing up in a foreign country and being somewhat of a sensitive child also played a part. "I've always found reading history — if it's well-written — to be exciting. It's all the greatest stories which have ever unfolded, and I find all that sex and violence pretty riveting."

Thus, Peter returned to the United States in the 1960s to study history at Dartmouth University. "I was an early supporter of the Vietnam war," Peter now ruefully admits. "I'd been in the Far East, and believed strongly that the communists had to be stopped — but I gradually became opposed to the war as a direct result of the American Civil Rights Movement."

"I can remember my father reading *Time* magazine while we were still back in the Philippines — and his outrage at how Birmingham's Chief of Police Bull Connor had turned the firehoses on the black protestors in Alabama — and how black people in general were being treated in the United States by their own government."

"I personally became radicalized by an incident where a black man witnessed the senseless murder of another black by a powerful local politician in Mississippi. The black man attempted for a number of days to just forget about it — knowing that there would be no justice — but could not. His conscience just wouldn't let it go. He was afraid of going to the local police because some of them were Klansmen, so instead he went to the FBI in Jackson — and the FBI promptly informed the politician of the charges. When the black man returned to his farm, the politician was waiting. The black man knew what was going to happen, and attempted to hide under his pick-up truck. But the good-ole-boy politician — in full view of the black man's family — killed him dead with a shotgun. And nothing happened. *That's* what made me a radical."

"At the time, the southern States seemed so retrograde," said Peter. "People were dying, and nobody seemed to care. So black leaders of the civil rights movement asked white volunteers from the north for their help. The idea was that maybe southern cops could kill blacks without fear of legal repercussions — but they couldn't treat whites quite the same way. So we white people acted as a sort of buffer between the black protesters and the police. The presence of the whites — many of us came from wealthy or influential families — forced the FBI to protect the rights of all the civil rights workers. And, the plan worked. It was a good call. It helped."

Back at Dartmouth, Peter became increasingly active in the anti-war movement. With the help of another radical student, he founded the Dartmouth chapter of the Students for a Democratic Society (SDS). Along the way, he collected his degree in history.

Then Nixon came along. "In 1968, Nixon was elected. Supposedly, he had a secret plan to end the war. The plan turned out to be outrageous. He bombed the hell out of Hanoi, and invaded both Cambodia and Laos. That's when I left the States. I was disgusted."

"By that time I'd fallen in love, and married my wife Dorothy. We arrived in St. John during hurricane season in 1968. We had a knapsack full of books — mostly Marxist — and a hundred bucks. We pitched a tent on the beach in Cinnamon Bay, and watched the sailboats glide by. I remember thinking what a beautiful spot it was, and how nice it would be to own a boat here."

Soon Peter and Dorothy met Guy Benjamin, Herman Sprauve, and other local West Indian 'bahn heer' residents. "Everyone was so warm and friendly," said Peter. "We were charmed by the local people and their culture. Everybody smiled at everyone, and it was so peaceful. Everyone greeted each other and chatted when they met. Dorothy left her purse on the ferry dock, and it was still there untouched the following day. We loved the fish-frys and the music."

Peter's plan had originally been to return to New York, save up enough money to buy a jeep, drive the jeep to Brazil, and join the revolution there. But St. John seemed too magical to leave. "Lucky for us, there was a desperate need for teachers. The courts had just handed down an order instructing the VI government to provide schooling for all the children of alien workers — so there was a suddenly a huge boom in the school population. So Herman Sprauve suggested we become school teachers — and we did."

Both Peter and Dorothy taught for a number of years at the Julius E. Sprauve School in Cruz Bay. "By that time, we'd bought a boat. We paid it off teaching school in the day, teaching night school, and working odd jobs. The boat's name was *Venceremos*. That was one of Che Guevara's favorite saying. It means 'we will win' or 'we shall overcome.' At the time, there was only one other live-aboard boat in Cruz Bay — that was John and Jean Mason on *Six Pence*. Then Art Albright on *Kuling* dropped his hook. Everybody on the island knew us, and we knew everybody. It was a wonderful time.

"I hate to use the term 'golden age' but it seems that way looking back on those days. Maybe because we were young and it was all so new and fresh. The water was clear as blue light, the fry were so thick they formed black clouds in the sea, and lobster crawled all over the reefs. On land it was exciting to be living in the West Indies with its vibrant way of life. The Mighty Sparrow was still in his prime, his songs everywhere on the radio and people's lips. Bob Marley and reggae were coming up strong with a new musical ethos that put the West Indies front and center on the world stage. At the fish-frys and in the bars and the park black and white mingled easily. There were fewer continentals here then, and they enjoyed participating in Caribbean culture. It was vital, open, earthy, imbued with old-fashioned values — honesty, respect, hard work, spiritual belief. The island was also booming economically and the intoxication of prosperity made everyone optimistic. The hangover was yet to come.

"We had a motorscooter at the time, and we'd always be tooling around. Dorothy would ride on the back, and our new baby boy, Rafael, would be sandwiched in between. Our method of transportation was somewhat frowned upon. People on the island felt a scooter was too dangerous a vehicle to carry a small child. Once we had a minor accident, and ran off the road. Dorothy's foot was injured. It wasn't too serious, but it was bleeding. The baby and I were fine. Madaleine Sewer happened to be driving to school. She spotted us, stopped, and drove us to the clinic. Once there, Miss Myrah Keating Smith took in the whole situation with a single glance. She immediately grabbed the baby, got down on her knees, and held him up to heaven. 'Thank you, Lord, for protecting this child' she prayed. That accomplished, she then attended to Dorothy's foot. That's how it was done back in those days — first the Lord, and then the first aid kit."

Of course, Peter still took his political beliefs seriously. When President Nixon came to Caneel Bay to relax during the Nam War, Peter — with the help of his friend Andy Rutnik — sailed a boat back-and-forth in front of the beach with sails which read "While Nixon lazes, Indo-China blazes!" The Secret Service was not amused.

The "cause" was clearly still important to Peter. However, it seemed the more Peter fell in love with St. John, the more his world view mellowed. He still held strong beliefs, but he was gradually tempering his outspokenness.

"Teaching school was a good way to get involved in the community and get to know people. Back in those days a teacher on St. John was a person who commanded great respect. Miss Clarice Thomas kind of exemplified the profession. She was the principal of Julius Sprauve School then and she had taught for fifty years. She was a sweet soul. She was very quiet, retiring, and fragile — she must have been close to 70 in those days — but when she'd come into a classroom the students would immediately hush. You could hear a pin drop. There was a tremendous respect for her. She had taught the kids, their parents, and their grandparents — she'd taught way back when it was just a one room school. She was a principled person who gave a lot to the community."

"I also had to admire teachers like Mr. Melville Samuel. He had such a positive attitude towards teaching. He was strong yet gentle, strict but humorous, always proper while a twinkle in his eyes put you at ease. The guy was a great role model for his third grade class which included my son Raffy one year.

"I liked the math teacher too, Mr. Sprauve. A very nice guy, quiet but in complete control of his class, which lived in awe of him. He loved boats and fishing and had a sleek, fast Tortola boat moored in Cruz Bay. We used to talk about fishing and the sea. I remember him telling me about his rowing to St. Thomas and back one night when he was a teenager, all to see a girlfriend.

"I enjoyed my classes, but I sometimes had my difficulties. I was not a very good disciplinarian. Junior high kids can be tough, and I didn't have a lot of training or experience. Part of the problem was a culture gap. Teachers had always been community pillars and West Indian teachers dressed accordingly. We young white hippies had quite different attitudes about dress. I was pretty casual. I wore the same ratty old tie and a pair of beat up sandals. The kids constantly deplored the sandals, so finally I broke down and bought a brand new pair of shoes. When I wore them into the classroom for the first time, the kids actually stood up and cheered. Only a week later baby Raffy dropped them over the side in the murky harbor at Coral Bay to see what would happen — he loved to see the splash — and when I returned to school in sandals the students were dismayed.

"I think I had a couple of exceptionally bright classes. Many of the students went on to college and careers in the states. I taught Karen Samuel, for instance. She and her sister Carmen used to sit together, like pretty little angels, always polite and attentive, always with their lessons mastered. The class from long habit turned to them to do the artwork to decorate the classroom at Christmas time. Now it's great to see what a fine artist Karen has become.

"I taught Alberto Samuel too. He went on to become an exemplary teacher who eventually taught my two sons at the Guy Benjamin School in Coral Bay. Both Raffy and Diego thought he was terrific. I thought that was a nice continuum, illustrative of the way things are on a small island."

Despite the affection that Peter has for St. John, he was also intrigued by offshore sailing and the cruising life. A boat seemed the perfect method of transportation to travel the Caribbean in search of adventure.

"Dorothy and I cruised down-island on *Venceremos*. The boat was a wooden 27 foot marconi rigged cutter built in Africa. Even though the boat was pretty small, we had a swell time. On St. Barts we met Lou Lou Magras, and began our life-long friendship. We cruised up and down the Lesser Antilles, and we met a multitude of wonderful people."

It was during this time that Peter became a seasoned sailor, and a man of the sea. Yes, he was a radical, yes, he loved St. John — but the ocean's horizon called. And, like many men before him, Peter found that its call could not be denied.

He decided to return to St. John, and build a boat capable of sailing anywhere in the world. While his wife Dorothy helped found Pine Peace School and raise their two sons Rafael and Diego, Peter did just that.

"Quite a few people told me I was nuts to build out in Coral Bay, but I don't regret my decision," said Peter. "So many people in the community helped us, encouraged us, and believed in us. I'm not sure I could have pulled it off in Miami or Fort Lauderdale."

Peter built his boat at Round Bay on the East End of St. John. He started her in 1979, and launched her in 1982 — using logs, a back-hoe, and lots of friends to push her into the water. Her length over-all is 49 feet, length on deck is 42 feet, and she draws 6 1/2 feet. She weighs 18 tons normally — almost 21 tons when she is fully loaded for an ocean passage. She's ketch rigged, and flies more than 1200 square feet of sail.

Although Peter and Dorothy did 99% of the work — they are both quick to point out how much help they received from St. Johnians. At the launching/celebration in June of 1982, dozens of community members helped load the lead ballast aboard as soon as she was floated.

Peter and Dorothy named their new boat *Breath*. She was — and is — an extremely rugged double-ended airex-cored fiberglass gaff-rigged ketch designed by Paul Johnson. If you wanted to charter a boat to sail off the edge of the earth — this would be an ideal choice.

Dorothy, Peter, and their two sons did, indeed, charter *Breath*. They catered to a more rugged, down-to-earth clientele than some of the 'goldplater' charter yachts.

For many of their guests, chartering *Breath* was the sailing experience of a lifetime. Dorothy dished out superb meals from the galley, even baking pies for dessert as they sailed. Peter literally taught them 'the ropes', and regaled them with a million sea stories. It wasn't just a charter; it was an Authentic Experience.

"Once we chartered to three doctors," said Peter. "I'd wake 'em all up at dawn to cat up our main anchor. One of them like to yell, 'I hate this!' — but he really loved it. He ended up giving slide shows of the trip at medical conferences."

Peter's charter guests — though occasionally wary of his world views at first — often fell under Peter's magic spell. Peter is such an open, honest, and straight-forward fellow that it is difficult to resist his unaffected charm.

St. John resident Kathy Hilliard is a real estate manager who often sends charter guests to Peter. "They always have a great time," she jokes, "but... you know... they usually come back with the 'Peter is God' complex... It takes a few days for it to wear off..."

The Muilenburg family sailed numerous times to Venezuela, the Bahamas, and the States. They learned as they went. The sea is a strict and unforgiving teacher, but they managed. To survive, they slowly learned their lessons the hard way.

In 1989, Peter, Dorothy and sons set off on their Dream Cruise to Europe. "We were twenty-one days to the Azores," said Peter nonchalantly. "No problem."

Still an enthusiastic history buff, Peter wintered in Seville, Spain so he could do some archival research on the Caribbean. "I was able to actually hold some of our early history in my hands," Peter said. "Once I was reading a tattered letter that the Governor of Santo Domingo had sent back to Spain — and realized with a start that the two pirates he was complaining about were John Hawkins and Sir Francis Drake! The letter seemed to vibrate in my hand..."

They chartered in the Med — stopping in Italy, Greece, Turkey, and many other countries. "I loved the Med; loved cruising in Europe. It's like sailing through history..."

The cruising life was often interesting, and occasionally far too exciting. "One evening about midnight in a harbor in Africa, we struck an overhead power cable. The whole boat lit up in a bright-blue-ball of crackling electricity. Two of the kids were blown overboard into the water by the brute force of the electrical energy. Our dog — screaming with sparks blazing in his coat — jumped into the sea. Numerous fires broke out belowdecks..."

Amazingly, everyone survived. Even the dog turned up five miles down the coast, living a life of luxury in a fancy seaside resort.

They spent considerable time in Africa. "We went hundreds of miles up the Gambia river into the interior. We were amazed that most people — even the people who spoke many languages and were highly educated — believed in magic. They wore amulets made by their priests. They believed that certain amulets protected them from injury by guns or knives. When we expressed our disbelief, a special Marabou priest came aboard. He jabbed a broken beer bottle into his stomach repeatedly without injury. To prove he was also protected against metal, he borrowed one of our sharp knives, and started jabbing it into his arm. At first, nothing happened — and then the blood started pouring out of his wound... I rushed for bandages... one of the African fellows fainted... we were all in a state of total shock."

"The priest never showed any sign of pain; he never complained or offered any excuses. It was obvious that he just couldn't *believe* that the knife had actually cut him..."

During their passage back across the Atlantic Ocean to the Lesser Antilles — fifteen days of diminishing gales — they ran out of propane cooking fuel. "The kids were attempting to heat up food on our kerosene camp lamps," said Peter. "It didn't work too well. I fasted the last four days, and we all celebrated landfall in Sint Maarten at Burger King."

Their next stop was Cuba, where Peter got his first chance to see the results of his hero Fidel Castro's policies. "There is a lot wrong with Cuba, but there is also a lot *right* with it. Health care is universal. The school system has made illiteracy a thing of the past. And, whether Americans want to believe it or not, most of the Cuban people still believe in Castro as a leader. I think that history will treat him far kinder than we suspect."

The middle name of one of Peter's sons is Fidel.

After their Cuba cruise in 1991, Peter and Dorothy once again settled down in Coral Bay. She returned to teaching at Pine Peace School, and Peter began occasionally chartering *Breath*.

He also started turning his hobby of writing into a profession — and began having his stories appear in such respected publications as SAIL, Americas, and Reader's Digest.

"St. John has changed quite a bit," says Peter. "In the old days it was more cohesive. It had a unified style and culture which it lacks today. The traditional leaders were there. The kids, for the most part, were respectful. It all functioned more smoothly. At that point in time the fabric of society hadn't been distorted by the hordes of a new competing culture flocking down — people like me — white continentals. We've changed the feel of this place, changed the structure. And a lot of the changes, I can't help but feel, have not been improvements.

"Before, West Indian culture was dominant, and we newcomers fit into it. The native people were model hosts, adamantly opposed to any kind of racial bullshit, whatever the source. Black radicals from the states preaching anti-white sentiments ran into a brick wall down here.

"Now St. John has two cultures and to a great extent they're in competition for power. When we arrived there was no alternative to living within the West Indian community. If you didn't like it you left. Now a newcomer can move down to the island and rarely have to deal with West Indians. They can operate within the white culture that has grown here over the years. And that means a different type of continental can feel at home here, people who know nothing — and couldn't care less — about the local culture. It wasn't like that 25 years ago. We have a lot more polarization and resentment today because of it. The West Indians see their control over their home being eroded — by what has been a traditional enemy, the white man. Their hospitality has been betrayed... or so it seems.

"Of course, that's just one factor. No continentals ever moved down here with the idea of disinheriting anybody. They were attracted by the natural beauty and wanted to escape the pressure and hustle of urban stateside life. And the influx of tourists and affluent homebuilders has brought an unprecedented level of prosperity to the islands and turned a great many St. Johnians into affluent middle class folks.

"At this point I think that unplanned, unlimited development is definitely not in the best interests of the island. We should learn from Bermuda which has imposed limits to growth. In Bermuda every family is allowed one car only. People use buses and taxis and motorbikes, and traffic is not a problem. I think we should explore ways of encouraging local investment by people already here, pursue small guesthouses with local ambiance, rather than look to stateside conglomerates for funds to build more hotels. In Greece and Turkey most tourism is small scale, family-owned and the profits go directly to the local people. We need to look in that direction, not towards Miami Beach.

"It's tough to talk about race... it's venturing onto a mine-field boobytrapped by the past. The subject is, by common agreement, almost taboo in mixed company. It has too much potential to come out wrong. Different cultures don't always communicate clearly — that's inherent in diversity. Thus, certain types of behavior which whites perceive as racist, actually isn't — and vice-versa. Racial tension begets itself. You're treated rudely by someone — if that person is a different race you immediately think, aha... racist! If the rude person was your own race you'd be saying, 'damn jackass!' In the final analysis, race is irrelevant, it's the clash of cultures. Affluent black continentals have the same difficulties assimilating into the West Indian culture as white continentals do... maybe more.

"Despite its current problems, its growing pains, St. John remains one of the loveliest places in the world with a lot of good people. It isn't what it was, but neither is anywhere else. For the tail end of the troubled twentieth century, it's doing pretty well on all fronts... economically, ecologically, socially. We have our share of tension, but it may be a creative tension that leads to something new under the western sun... an equitable, mellow multi-racial society."

Cap'n Fatty Goodlander (aka Gary Martin Goodlander) regularly writes for a wide variety of local, national, and international publications. His two books, "Seadogs, Clowns, and Gypsies" and "Chasing the Horizon" have been reprinted numerous times. He currently lives aboard his 38 foot sloop Wild Card *with his wife Carolyn and daughter Roma Orion in Great Cruz Bay, St. John. He is also the founder of American Paradise Publishing.*

Gerda Marsh, My Great Great Aunt

by
Shurna Rabsatt

School: Ivanna Eudora Kean High
Grade: Tenth
Assignment: An Oral History

Class: Honors English
Student Age: 15
Teacher: Amy Roberts

My Great-Great-Aunt Gerda Marsh is 88 years old. She lives in Coral Bay, St. John. I visited her on a cool Sunday afternoon in January of 1992.

When I arrived at her house to interview her, she was busy doing her laundry. I sat on a chair and waited. After awhile I got up and looked around. There were faded photographs on the walls, and I longed to know the story behind every face. The room was filled with antiques. It was sort of dark inside because the living room door was shut. Streaks of sunlight beamed through a pair of old fashioned windows.

I decided to open the door and allow the sunlight in. I turned the knob, but the door wouldn't open. I wondered why. Then I remembered that her locks weren't like modern locks. You had to pull a chain with a little circle attached to it and lift up.

I turned the knob and stepped onto the porch. There were plants, old wooden chairs, tables and mildewed books scattered about. There was also a copper object called a "goose neck" which had once been used at the Carolina Estate during the Sugar Mill Era.

Looking into the big yard, I observed green grass, flowers and trees. Among them stood a perfect-sized pine tree. As I looked at this impressive tree — standing so tall and upright — it reminded me of my Great-Great-Aunt Gerda.

I noticed the door to the basement and wondered what other treasures lay beyond it. As I wondered, my eyes caught hold of what seemed to be a very old tree. It is called a "Taboli" tree, also locally known as yellow cedar. I later learned that this tree was planted by Aunt Gerda's father, who was my great-great-grandfather. He had brought a slip of the tree over from a place called Mosquito Estate in St. Thomas. It was the first tree of its kind on St. John. (Mosquito Estate now known as Lindberg, and is near the airport.)

With the sun shining on the yard and the little bananaquits and butterflies flying from tree to tree — the yard looked very peaceful.

I decided to go inside and roam around the house some more. I was becoming intrigued with my surroundings. One of the bedrooms contained an interesting old trunk. There was also a steel-framed bed painted turquoise, and two wooden cabinets with mesh-covered doors.

I walked across the wooden floor to peek into the next room. It contained almost all the same items, but here I felt a peculiar sense of *liking*. I didn't know what it was at the time, but I could sense immediately that this room was special. It wasn't until later that my aunt told me that this was where her parents had slept and spent their last days. Just rocking in their rocking chair made everything seem so peaceful and quiet. In a way, I didn't want to leave.

After awhile I walked into my aunt's room, which was filled with even more antiques. I looked at her bed. It had a net covering over it to protect her from mosquitoes. She had many old and wonderful things in her room. As I walked back to the living room, I wondered why old things fascinated me so much.

I suddenly wanted to remember all the stories my aunt used to tell me — all the fun times we had together over the years. Almost everyday my sisters and I used to go to her house for special candy that she made (and sold). We'd keep her company. She used to give us cookies and sodas and then sit us down and tell us some stories about the old days. Those were some good times. And now, while interviewing her, I was able to relive those times again.

It all began in Coral Bay at a gospel group. Two people met and fell in love. Ernest Marsh played in the orchestra. Minerva Marsh was one of the choralers. They had a baby girl named Gerda on April 9, 1906. More babies followed. Mr. Marsh died of kidney failure in 1935, and Mrs. Marsh died of a heart attack in 1945. They had ten children — Beatrice, Claymet, Dassie, Nellorine, Gerda, Egbert, Will, Ernest, Ivo and Florence. Now they have all passed away, except for Gerda.

Auntie Gerda said that she had a good relationship with her parents. Musically, she took after her dad by playing the church organ on Sundays.

All of her siblings were much alike, except for Ivo, one of the twins who she favored because he was frequently sick with epilepsy and was in pain. She recalled the time when her brothers and sisters all went out horseback riding. While trotting along, Ivo had one of his attacks. She had to hold him up and slow his horse down and at the same time try to stay on her own horse. She was both saddened and relieved when Ivo passed away; he was often in such misery. (My great grandfather, Ernest, was Ivo's twin.)

Gerda said her teenage years were all right. She found no fault with her parents. She had good relationships with her nine brothers and sisters though some weren't from the same parents.

Gerda attended a private school. In the Moravian Mission Church she learned writing, reading, arithmetic, social studies and science, but as she got into higher grades, she began to hate algebra. After high school she went to Antigua where she attended a female teachers' training college, but only spent a couple of years there.

As a young lady she was very active. She was captain of the cricket team and a teacher at the Boys Home in Leinster Bay. (The ruins of the Boys Home, now within the boundaries of the National Park, are still visible.) She taught there for 12 years. She was a very strict person and gained much respect as a teacher. Her motto was "Let them know what is right and what is wrong from the beginning." She also taught at Guy Benjamin, John's Folly, and East End on the Little Lookout Point.

Her teaching career ended because of conflicts of interests developed between her and the principal. Three days after she resigned, while sweeping off her stairs, she learned she'd been recommended for a job as a social worker by Ms. Verne Bornn. She was soon back at work, this time on St. Thomas. She rode a horse into Cruz Bay daily.

Gerda said that she always acted the way she did (so independent and truly responsible) because that's the way her parents had acted. She had a lot of things in her life because the Marshes were, and always have been, a prominent, respected family who supported the community. The Marshes were the first family in Coral Bay to open a shop. They sold candy, meat, goodies and more. The store was called "The Marsh's Grocery". They also had a big sailing cargo boat called the *Adella*. It brought supplies back and forth from St. Thomas. The store was destroyed when a man put fire to it.

Gerda didn't always live in the house that I described. She once lived in a four-story wooden house up on Carolina Hill. It got blown down by a terrible hurricane in 1924.

"Tonight we're in for it," said my Aunt Gerda's papa, who could tell a storm was coming from the change in the weather elements. They started barring up windows until they reached the fourth floor.

"Let's get away from up here," said her papa.

Gerda said, "Where are we going to go?"

Her papa said, "I don't know!"

They went to the basement. The storm worsened and the house

began to fall apart. They prayed that the Lord would be watching over the Marshes.

When the house didn't fall in and crush them — despite severe damage to its footings and one of its wooden walls being blown away in the storm — they knew the Lord was there.

After the storm was over they took refuge in the church where they met several other homeless families. They didn't stay long because while they were living in the church, Mr. Marsh was clearing out space to build the house that Gerda presently lives in. She never married because she never found anyone she loved enough.

During Gerda's long life she was presented with many awards. She's had a long, bountiful life. In 1932 she represented the Virgin Islands at the Atlantic City Fair in the United States.

As I listened to one of the stories she didn't want me to put into this interview, I studied her face closely. I noticed all the blue-gray lines within her hazel eyes as she recalled the distant past. I saw kindness and warmth in those eyes.

I asked her what she does around the house each day. She said, "Time is always taken up with something. There's seldom time to rest." In her younger days she baked, sewed, washed, made her own pillows and bedspreads. She also represented immigration and customs and social welfare in the Coral Bay area.

About five years ago, she got a TV. She enjoys watching it, but as a child was content without it. There was much for her to do around the house. "TV is for afterwards," she says.

She was never really alone since she had her six cats, including two Siamese, that kept her company.

We came to the close of our interview. I asked her about St. John twenty years ago. She said, "It hasn't changed that much except for more rum shops, businesses and houses." After that she got up to go stop the washer. I sat there for awhile wondering what her younger days must have been like.

It's strange. When I am in her house I want to know everything about her. I always thought when you reach your 80's that you would have to use a cane, hearing aid, and have poor eyesight, but Auntie Gerda doesn't need any of that. She looks like she still has a lot of years left in her.

During my visit I wanted to get more than just an interview on a sheet of paper. I wanted to venture through her mind; discover what she thinks, sees and dreams. She's a very wise woman. While visiting with her it is easy to understand why so many people love her. I do.

Shurna Rabsatt is a 16 year old student at Ivanna Eudora Kean High School in Red Hook. She is the daughter of Antonio Rabsatt and Jacquelyn Clendinen, and the sister of Iesha, India and Tia Rabsatt. She plans to attend college and possibly major in the human services and seek a career in journalism. "Special thanks to Amy Roberts, my English teacher, for helping me recognize and improve my writing skills, and the Almighty," she says.

She Did It With Donkeys

by Lito Valls

A brief sketch of Ethel W. McCully 1886 - 1980

The first time I saw "Grandma Raised the Roof McCully," as I later referred to her behind her back, was at the St. John Fourth of July Parade in 1972. Ethel Tvalbridge McCully, emigre from Manhattan's East Side Silkstocking District, was sitting on the sidewalk stoop near "Mooie's Bar" sipping and waiting for the parade which in those days lasted all of five minutes. Grandma was in good company, for squatting on the stoop with her was "His Excellency" former Governor John David Merwin.

Grandma was not always in good company. Very often when she got bored and the ennui of living alone at her self-designed and built 'Island Fancy' would set in, she hired the first passing Tortola sloop for St. Thomas where she proceeded to play "grandma" to the boys from whatever naval ship was visiting St. Thomas for the week-end. "Grandpa," most of the time was Archdeacon Swenson, Rector of All Saints Church. The story, probably apocryphal, is told that one evening a young Catholic sailor, not knowing he was approaching an Anglican divine, quietly asked Fr. Swenson for permission to walk him home as he thought he'd had enough. To which he yelled across the bar, "No shit!"

Ethel, as she was known to her close friends and associates, had come to St. John after abandoning a Tortola-bound boat and swimming ashore. She fell in love with (and later bought) a plot of land at Little Maho Bay also known as Mary Point. She re-named her portion "Island Fancy." After great travail of designing, planning and constructing a complex which included servants quarters, generator house and beach house, at a time when the only modes of transportation on St. John were horses, mules and donkeys, she raised her roof in 1953.

Mrs. McCully, who had tried her hand at mystery story writing and given up after three novels, decided to write again. This time she wrote about her great adventure of building her house on St. John. "Grandma Raised the Roof" was the title the publisher insisted for her book, much to her chagrin. She had wanted to call it, "I Did It With Donkeys."

Before giving up on her mystery story writing career, she had been an ambulance driver in World War I. Some of her works included: "Death Rides Tandem," "Doctors Beware," and "Blood on Nassam's Moon."

Although she gave up writing, she continued to attend the mystery-story writers convention and always came back home complaining that she was never able to get the award for the oldest living writer attending. "There's an old fart there that refuses to die!"

Longevity was one of her main topics of conversation. Not long after she had returned from a trip to China, hard on the heels of Kissinger and Nixon, she took over the "QE II" to do 90 days around the world. Quite appropriate, since she was 90 years old at the time. "Tell me about your trip," I said to her upon her return. "I'm sure you had a wonderful time." "Wonderful time my eye," she said, "the youngest man on the boat was seventy!"

"Grandma Raised the Roof McCully" was at various times my neighbor both at Mary Point and in Cruz Bay. Her "town house" was a small cottage near the beach where she spent two nights a week. Wednesday night was "de rigueur" dinner at "Eric's Hill Top," where she kept court for locals, tourists and snow-birds alike. One evening she made her way home in a torrential downpour — soaked to the gills, galoshes on feet, flashlight in hand. I accosted Eric Christian, her host, for not bringing Mrs. McCully home in the downpour, to which he replied, "I offered to take her home and she was highly insulted because, as she said, I thought she was some old ninny."

Occasionally at Island Fancy she would have me over for cocktails, and as she sipped snifter after snifter of Napoleon brandy, she snickered, "Dr. Tobacco says I'm allowed four ounces of brandy a day, but he didn't say how often."

Her cache of brandy was continuously replenished by her "Admirals" on the "Spanish Armada" or the "Puerto Rican Navy" as she liked to call the flotilla of power boats from Puerto Rico that anchored on her bay on long week-ends. "They've never bothered me," she kept saying. "All I do is row over in my dinghy, introduce myself and join the party."

From the "Admirals" of the Spanish Armada to the local constabulary and the National Park officials, Ethel had a way of disarming authority. One warm afternoon after a Fourth of July Parade in Cruz Bay, some of us living in the Mason's compound realized we had been victims of a robbery, an almost unheard-of thing in those days. Sergeant Alphonse Powell and his aides were summoned. Sergeant Powell was a no nonsense officer, known to take money out of his own pocket and ship-off any bums coming off the ferries, right back to St. Thomas. He was conducting a serious investigation when Ethel decided to call off the whole inquiry by waving the officers away with, "I don't know what we're all worried about a few pennies and items lost; it could have been worse. We could have been raped!" To which the sergeant chivalrously responded, "You still have hopes?"

Another occasion when Mrs. McCully had a run-in with uniformed authority was when a cadre of National Park Rangers from the Regional Office in Atlanta descended upon Island Fancy to try to talk her into paying rent. Grandma had sold her house to the Park and retained a life tenancy. "Well, you know Mrs. McCully," said the rangers, "this house now belongs to the park and you're going to have to pay some kind of rent even if it's only a nominal sum." Ethel, never at a loss for words, ricocheted: "RENT? According to the actuarial tables, I'm supposed to be dead! How are you going to collect rent from a dead woman?"

Of course she never paid any rent, taxes or garbage collection fees. Her Christmas card that year was a painting of herself in a lame dress, swinging in her hammock, with a long cigarette holder. A peacock on one side, a donkey on the other, and a park ranger tacking up a sign "U.S. PROPERTY" on her house. The caption? "You can so have your cake and eat it too! MERRY CHRISTMAS."

Grandma always had a flare for doing things her own way. For example, her Island Fancy did not have a living room as such. Instead she had the most elegantly furnished porch with elaborate wicker and wrought iron furniture, wrought iron balconies and crystal chandeliers. She invented and designed her own coat-of-arms replete with goats, donkeys and peacocks and had it executed by well-known St. Thomas artist, Ira Smith. It was emblazoned with her motto: "WE HATE PROGRESS"

She hated "progress" to the point where she went all out fighting the establishment of the Maho Bay Campground in her own front yard. She berated the St. Thomas authorities for granting the permit to build and accused them of attempting to mess up St. John after they had "fouled-up" their own nest. Nevertheless, she was a good sport, and after she realized what an ecological show place Maho had turned out to be, she went over to the inauguration and danced and drank Monty Jack, the manager, under the table.

Needless to say, Grandma never missed a party and always insisted in bringing her own water and her own ice, even to

Government House receptions, for, as she maintained, her stomach was no longer made of cast iron. Grandma was always the life of the party even when everyone there was young enough to be her grandchild. One memorable evening she stole the show completely as some lizard eggs which had been nesting in her wig decided to hatch and leap all over the place, much to the delight of all the party-goers who swore that Ethel had planned the whole thing.

Unknown to her, I learned a few lessons from Mrs. McCully. The most important one perhaps was never to eat on the run. Both in town and in the country I observed how meticulously she set her table for breakfast, lunch and dinner, as if she were expecting Queen Elizabeth to sup. And after she had taken care of the "mise en place," she would sit down and eat in solitary splendor.

Stories about "Grandma Raised the Roof McCully" are rife among St. John taxi-drivers. Camile Paris likes to tell the one about taking her home one late afternoon in the days when the dirt road on the northside ended at the Maho Bay Goat Trail, still in existence as an entrance to the campground. As it was getting pretty dark, Paris helped her light her lantern which was kept hidden in the bushes. As he rounded the curb overlooking Maho Bay and Island Fancy on his way back, he stopped to look for the lantern winding its way up the hill. No lantern. Three days later when he saw her in town he inquired the reason. "Oh, for goodness sake," she said. "I was in no condition to go home then. I went for a swim, then took a nap on the beach and then about two o'clock in the morning I went home." Richie Penn likes to tell the one about how she hated anyone to assist her by the elbow while getting into a jeep or safari bus. "Unhand me," she would grumble, "I'm no old lady!" One day she fell to the ground. So Richie said to her, "Pick yourself up since you're no old lady." Which she promptly did, laughing all the way back to the goat trail. Oliver "Tom" Samuel's story is about the time he went to pick her up after she had spent $14,000 paving her very steep driveway. The driveway, newly-finished, was not passable, so he walked down to her gate to meet her and help her up the rough terrain. "Just carry the cooler," she said. "I can handle myself." Then she mumbled all the way up the steep driveway that she hoped the workers had done a good job, as she intended to be around a long time to enjoy it.

Alas, Ethel did not live long enough to enjoy her driveway. For she died soon after and was buried at sea on the fifth of January 1981. True to her own indomitable self, she made arrangements to have a good old fashioned wake party at Caneel. About five years before she had held a dry-run so all could learn exactly how she wanted it done.

As with everything she did in life, she never gave-up and never gave-in. The night before she died she had spent her time dancing at Caneel Bay until two o'clock in the morning.

God bless you, Grandma, wherever you are.

Author Lito Valls is profiled by Amy Roberts elsewhere in this book.

Karen Samuel

by

Cap'n Fatty Goodlander

Karen Samuel lives in a big white house atop a small windswept hill in sleepy Coral Bay. Her childhood home, the Estate Eden house, is just a stone's throw away to the west. She is a small, compact, graceful, attractive, soft-spoken 34 year old woman — with impeccable manners and a gentle demeanor — who quietly describes herself as "shy and reclusive."

To say that Karen's local roots go back a long way is to make a vast understatement. Her mother, Doris E. Callwood, is from nearby Tortola. Her family has been involved with the Arundel Rum Distillery for some 250 years. Karen's father, Willis O. Samuel, can trace his roots back almost 300 years on St. John. (The Samuels have always been a well-respected and important family on St. John. He was an overseer for Herbert Lockhart at the Leinster Bay Estates before it was sold to the National Park.)

Because of all the above facts, it would be easy to jump to the conclusion that Karen is a typical modern West Indian housewife whose personal horizons are primarily focused on her family's property, her husband's job, and her children's growing pains.

Yes, that would be an easy stereo-typical assumption to make, and also a totally wrong one.

Karen is an internationally respected artist whose pictures are among the finest, most expensive "fine art" being produced in the Caribbean today.

"I paint in spurts. Right now I'm in a down cycle, but that won't last long. If I'm working on a series of paintings, I'll start 10 or 15 at once, and then finish them two or three at a time. I normally work from 8 till 4 or 5 in the afternoon. I can't work at night; the light is not right... especially since I'm a Caribbean artist whose work reflects the bright sky and clear colors of these islands."

As she speaks, she sits with perfect posture in a straight-backed white plastic chair on her sun-bleached front porch. There is a quiet and shady and lazy feeling in the summery air. Hummingbirds dart across the spacious yard. Frigate birds ride the thermals high above the roof. Chameleons do slow, spasmodic push-ups on the porch columns. Flies buzz by. The nor'eastern tradewinds push the entire sky of high fleecy clouds westward. An occasional mosquito whines through.

Each time the interviewer speaks, she looks directly at him. But when she replies, she looks away — as if to speak the truth requires a certain degree of anonymity from his inquisitive glance.

"Many of my customers prefer my landscapes. They sell well. But I feel some of my best paintings are of ordinary people doing ordinary things. Although they often don't sell as fast, these are the pieces that international collectors with money are most interested in.

"The anatomy of the face is so important; I have to get the muscles under the skin just right. I paint the eyes last. Sometimes I spend days and days and days just on the eyes. Yes, the eyes are the most important. If I get the eyes right, I've got it. They will draw you into the picture; they're direct windows to the soul."

Karen is a complex, complicated, highly motivated person. Her life-work of painting brings her such pleasure, and not a little pain. Like most artists, she requires a certain isolation and privacy to work — and this causes her to feel that the tiny distances between herself and her neighbors are widening, not shrinking.

"I'm never bored. I have endless projects I'm working on... endless *things* to do, but not... so many people in my life right now. I'm working at a certain level of intensity... that doesn't mesh with much of the social interaction here on St. John. I love it here, but, frankly, I sometimes think I should have stayed in the States after college — and been more challenged...

"You know, I have always believed in education. I have always loved school, admired my teachers and worked hard. I have been 'taught' a tremendous amount. But now I'm beginning to educate myself. I'm still in school, only this time I'm the teacher. I'm more challenging of ideas now, and less accepting. And I'm beginning to understand how complicated life can be..."

There's the paradox of Karen Samuel. She is fiercely proud of her family, her people, their history, her culture, this island. She has, since the cradle, been driven to excel. Her family, the church, and the schools all endlessly reinforced the message that she could be all that she wanted to be — *if* she worked hard and never lost sight of the goal.

She bought the program — lock, stock, and barrel. She read. She studied. She practiced. She followed the rules.

And it worked. Sort of.

She was everyone's darling — and has the faded photographs in the treasured dog-eared scrapbooks to prove it. Here's a shot of her first "one woman" art show at the VI Council of the Arts. Here she is accepting an award with Senator Virdin Brown. There is a blurry snapshot of St. John administrator Noble Samuel making a speech about her. Here is a copy of the letter informing her she has won the coveted scholarship...

One of the reasons Karen went to America was to test herself against the best — and, as expected, she did well. She studied at the Corcoran School of the Arts, and graduated from George Washington University.

Every step of the way, she earned the right to continue on to the next level of excellence by hard work, raw talent, and a total dedication to the cause.

Then she came back and taught art in the public school here for nine years.

"For the first five years, I worked so very, very hard," she said. "I was an extremely motivated teacher. I tailored my students' assignments according to their individual skill level, and made sure that each year I changed and improved my lesson plans based on my recent experience. I had some great students, and I like to think I did some good. But after nine years, I quit.

"Working for the government and the school system was... difficult. I couldn't get the proper art supplies for my students. You can only reach into your own pocket so often before it grates. I was trying to teach them to paint, but our brushes were useless. They wouldn't take the correct shape or spring back as they should. They shed hairs on every stroke. Everything was substandard. The paint, the paper — everything. You can't produce good art with inferior materials...

"It was so frustrating. I wanted my students to learn, to advance, to break through to the next level of technique...

...but in the end I realized that I wanted more for them than they wanted for themselves. So I quit."

Listening to Karen speak — despite the calm cadence of her soft muted words — is like putting your ear to the side of a serene mountain and hearing a volcano within. She is a simmering pot of pride, regret, hope, ambition, challenge, anger, dedication, love, fear, respect, and faith.

"What would I like for the people of St. John to think of me after I'm gone? I'm not sure. I seldom think how I'm perceived by others. I'd like them to think of me as a good person... as a person who contributed to this society, who cared. I'd like to think that some of my experiences in life might be uplifting to others....

"As one of the few serious native artists in the Virgins, I feel that I am somewhat of a role model for our youth whether I want to be or not. It is important to our youngsters to realize that you can achieve success and financial independence — not just the trappings of material success, but real success — by following your own vision. You don't have to submerge yourself into a larger group to succeed. It's important for them to realize that you can go your own way and succeed... that you should never allow others to limit what you become....

"But it often isn't easy. Especially for an artist. This society doesn't value art. It's not important here. People don't spend money on it. I don't know what the answer to this problem is — maybe there isn't one. But I do know that being an artist is a *true profession*. Art is what lasts, what projects a culture down through the ages. It's important.

"I'd like to think that, if I'm successful, I could set an example. Even if only a few kids picked up on it — even if it only made a significant difference in a couple of young lives — that would be enough.

"When I chose this career path, I didn't have any artistic example to follow... there were no successful role models to emulate. But this society *needs* its artists regardless of whether it realizes it or not.

"Art is where I make my stand," she says softly as she glances away. "The movement towards perfection is what makes life worth living."

The interior world of Karen Samuel is a richly diverse, intense, sophisticated one — but not necessarily an easy one. Her world view is filled with both light and shadow. Sometimes it seems as if she is flinging herself into the future while clinging to the past. She often appears to be caught between two worlds — West Indian and Continental, artistic and commercial, traditional and modern, spiritual and material.

But one thing that she is absolutely clear about is her childhood. "I had the most wonderful childhood imaginable," she says.

Karen was born on St. John on January 12th, 1959. She is one of ten children — Alberto, Avalino, Carmen, Coreen, Curtiss, Brenda, Christine, Ricardo, and Cicerly are her siblings.

Much of her early childhood was spent living with her Aunt Adina Callwood in Cane Garden Bay on Tortola. "We used play all day on the beach. We lived in swimsuits. We spent a lot of our time 'visiting' with each other. The Henleys and the Callwoods and other related families were all there right on the beach. It was an outdoor life. Most of the men were fishermen, and when they'd come in each day the women would cook up the catch...

"My father kept a boat in Leinster Bay which we traveled back and forth to Tortola on. The summer before kindergarten, I moved back to St. John permanently. I loved playing all day with my brothers and sisters, and a nearby aunt had seven kids... so everyone was pretty much family."

It was at this point that Karen discovered the library at the Moravian Church, and reinforced her life-long love affair with reading.

"My father was an avid reader," says Karen. "He had wanted to be a doctor, but had been forced to stay on St. John to help his family instead of going to college. In any event, he instilled in all his children a deep joy of reading."

There were chores, of course. While their father worked at Leinster Bay for Herbert Lockhart, the family had to take care of a large number of diverse tasks.

"We tended the garden and took care of the animals. We had cattle, horses, donkeys, goats, sheep, pigs, and chickens — you name it. But there were so many of us kids — and we had so much fun doing it — that it didn't seem like work. I especially remember moving the goats and sheep from pasture to pasture. That was always a fun day."

Karen found school exciting from the very beginning. "I attended the Ben Franklin School here in Coral Bay. The school has since been renamed the Guy Benjamin School. Guy Benjamin is my godfather. Anyway, when I was in second grade, they allowed me to complete two years of schooling in the space of one. I ended up in the same class as my older sister Carmen. I always loved school. Miss Eudora Marsh was principal then, and she was both very strict and very loving. Our public schools back in those days were quite good — heavily grounded in the fundamentals. Our teachers were very caring, socially conscious people, and we were proud of them and our schools.

"A school day would start out with the Pledge of Allegiance and the singing of the National Anthem. Next, we'd have to recite our multiplication tables. At the end the day, we'd say a prayer which began...

> Now the day is over
> Its night is drawing nigh
> Shadows of the evening
> Beam across the sky...

"I was brought up to believe that education was *the* most valuable asset a person could have," says Karen. "This was the message I got from my family, and it was reinforced by both my church and my school. Education was the key!"

Learning, of course, wasn't just confined to school and church for Karen. Learning was what life was all about. From her mother Doris, Aunt Ella Hodge, and others — Karen learned other equally important arts.

"We were taught to sew, knit, crochet, and embroider. My sister Carmen and I would sew Barbie (doll) outfits which we'd sell to other kids for a quarter — enough to buy a soda or popsicle on a hot day."

Both girls continued to do well in school — though a few of the Cruz Bay kids would refer to some of their fellow Coral Bay students as "bookies," a derogatory term which meant "simple country folk."

Spelling was one of Karen's favorite subjects, and she always won the spelling bees. It was during a particularly exciting spelling bee that she acquired her childhood nickname.

"I was excited, and squirming around because I knew the answers," recalls Karen with a faint, far-away smile of remembrance. "The teacher wanted me to calm down. 'Be still. Don't be so gippy,' the teacher said. That's how I got the nickname 'Gippy'. Some people still call me that, but not many. I hate it!"

Upon graduation from the ninth grade, Carmen was valedictorian and Karen was salutatorian. Bill Lomax, Beverly Barsel, Marianne Hedges, Roy Sewer, and Julius Sprauve are some of the teachers Karen remembers with special fondness.

"It was a little before this time when I started drawing — but it wasn't a part big part of my life. Actually, it wasn't until high school that I went to my first art class...."

The Ivanna Eudora Kean High School in Red Hook was named the Nazareth Bay School when Karen first attended the 10th grade there. Soon after becoming a student at the school, she was befriended by an African American art teacher from Georgia named Virginia Essex.

"She started allowing me to use acrylics, and tutoring me in oils. I was encouraged to do other art projects outside the class, and I even visited her at home. It began to dawn on me that I was getting special attention because of my drawing skills."

The school library displayed 15 of Karen's paintings. This was her first "art show." Then the VI Council of the Arts, Our Lady of Mount Carmel church, and other organizations asked to show her work — and she was on her way as a budding artist.

Then the VI Council of the Arts sent Karen and a dozen other VI students to the South Hampton College on Long Island (NY) for a month.

"That whole scene was just amazing to me. Here I was at 14 years old... away from home for the very first time... living in a co-ed dorm without an adult chaperon... and drawing nude models all day! I couldn't believe it. People were studying drawing, painting, design, pottery, sculpting..."

Karen found it an intoxicating experience, and probably one which has shaded the rest of her life. After high school, she again left St. John — this time to attend George Washington University. (The VI Council on the Arts again helped by granting Karen a partial scholarship to defray some of the cost of her tuition for the first two years.)

One of the reasons that Karen went away to college was to see how she'd measure up academically against the student body of a major, well-respected university. What she wasn't expecting was that the most challenging part of college was on the social side.

"I was 16, and suddenly discovered myself surrounded by a bunch of... (she struggles for softer modifiers but finally gives up) ...rich spoiled brats who were spending their $300.00 a week allowances while whining that they didn't have any pocket money. I couldn't believe it!

"Suddenly, I realized that I, at least in some ways, was poor. This had never dawned on me because I had always had what I needed. But these kids were living in a different economic world.

"This amazed and amused me at first, and then made me angry. Money, for the first time in my life, suddenly became important. Don't get me wrong — I wasn't deprived during my college days. There was plenty of free stuff to do, and we had fun. But if you didn't have money, it was often difficult go out and socialize in certain ways — not unless you wanted to mooch, and I *never* mooch! I sometimes had to turn down invitations simply because I couldn't afford to take part in them. It was depressing to be constantly surrounded by things you can't have... by events you can't engage in...

"...and the worst part is that.... somehow, I've never been able to fully shake that sense of... that sudden awareness of class consciousness."

But Karen and her sister Carmen persevered. They rolled up their sleeves and went to work. They became small-scale entrepreneurs. They worked summer jobs, sewed custom-made dresses for the other girls in the dorm, and even braided other students hair in corn-rows to earn spending money...

...and they got by. (Carmen earned a master's degree in Nutrition, returned to the VI to work at the St. Thomas Hospital for awhile, and is currently in North Carolina working on her doctorate.)

While her studies at the Corcoran School of the Arts were challenging, Karen wanted to learn far more than they offered. So she also enrolled in art classes at George Washington University.

"When I first began attending Gene Davis's classes at Corcoran, I didn't even know who he was. It turns out he's famous for paintings of stripes. Anyway, I needed someone to tell me which type of brush to use and how to mix my oils — and here I was surrounded by some of the best professional artists in world — established professional artists in their 50's and 60's — who were dripping drops of paint on canvas... and splattering... and jabbing... working on pieces of canvas ten by twelve feet across... and here I was drawing little realistic scenes of the English countryside...

"...I was too shy to say anything, too intimidated. I was totally on the wrong side of the trend towards abstract art — which has now reversed itself, lucky for me. But I certainly didn't fit in with that group..."

Despite being somewhat disappointed by her first experience at Corcoran, Karen had no thoughts of giving up. Her second class was on drawing, and she felt it was exactly what she needed. Then came anatomy...

"Suddenly I was getting the technical instruction I had longed for all my life. I learned that until you could draw the muscles of the human face without the skin, you were never going to be able to draw a proper face. I learned not to be too tight and controlled as I worked, but to be loose and flexible. I learned to draw with my whole arm, not just my wrist..."

After returning to St. John and spending nine years teaching, Karen quit in 1988. She summered in England that year, unwinding while deciding what to do next.

Then, during an unplanned visit to St. Croix, she met Kime Holman of New York. They fell in love and married.

"Starting the Coral Bay Folk Art Gallery at Wharfside Village in Cruz Bay was his idea," says Karen. "He's devoted three years of his life to it. The gallery has been good for us in a number of ways. It allows us to showcase our art and local crafts in an environment which is worthy of them, and has, at least to some degree, enhanced the cultural tourism aspect of St. John.

"We've certainly lifted up the level of presentation! No more 'art shows' of unframed canvas sitting on a cement floor...

"Also as a direct result of the gallery, I've signed a contract to illustrate a children's book and I have well-known international galleries displaying my works in the Soho district of New York City, New Jersey, California, and Hawaii.

"I'm not sure we'll stay in the retail business forever, but it has been an interesting experience. It has enabled me to meet a lot of people I would not otherwise have come in contact with, and to be forced to listen to their comments and criticisms of my paintings.

"I'm proud of the gallery and what it has accomplished, but also disappointed by the lack of local support. It is almost impossible to make a living with art on St. John unless you're a commercial graphic artist."

What does the future hold for Karen? She's not sure. Right now she's still interested in learning more about her craft. "I'm close to — but not quite — where I want to be technically as an artist. The life of an artist is a difficult one, and I'm slowly coming to terms with that. There's a price to pay if you're driven to creatively express yourself — and it's a big one.

"In school, everything was clear. If you worked hard and studied well, you won. I don't mean to sound too philosophical, but real life isn't like that. There's a lot of confusion. The pleasure and the pain is mixed together. What is right and what is wrong isn't always so clear.

"But I want to be a successful artist *here* — not just for myself — but also for the ones behind me.

"I love St. John. This is my home. These people are my family. But I don't like the direction of the trends taking place. The quality of life here is diminishing, not increasing. When I grew up, the public schools were nearly as good as the private. That's not true anymore. Kids today have a million material possessions but they seem to lack a lot of the basic values which are so important in life. We need quality, not quantity here on St. John. Our leaders aren't leaders — they only think in the short term. I wish we would come up with a good, solid, *long term* plan for our future. I think that some of the people of St. John have a desire to be more independent politically, to have more control over their own destinies. Progress? I'm not sure how much we've made in the last twenty years. We seem to have absorbed much of the negative aspects of other cultures — especially American culture — and very little of the positive..."

Karen speaks these words almost as if she is talking to herself, carrying on an interior monologue. Her head slowly shakes from side-to-side in reluctant agreement with her soft words. Her liquid brown eyes slowly slide away towards the horizon — now she is serenely looking out into the bright sunshine from the dark shadow of her own private, personal porch.

As the interviewer prepares to depart — picking up his papers, pad, and pencil — his last image of her is a silent black silhouette against the vivid green landscape.

Later that evening, he seeks out what he considers her best, most vivid painting — the one in which a West Indian market lady wears an apron labeled JOY. He stares at it for a long time. After awhile, the rest of the world seems to dissolve around him. It is just him and the painting. There is something about the painting which both enthralls and repels him. He can't figure it out. He loves the painting, and yet there is some element within it which makes him vaguely nervous.

He keeps focusing and unfocusing his eyes in an attempt to *feel* the painting versus just *observe* it.

And then, suddenly, it's just him and the Eyes.

There is pride in those eyes, and pain too. They're hoping for the best, but preparing for the worst. They are the eyes of a survivor. They have endurance. They don't give up. They are kind, loving, nurturing eyes — open, truthful, and caring eyes — but they also hold a faint hint of regret and sadness around the edges. And deep within these fathomless eyes is a well-concealed, seldom-glimpsed source of intense heat... the banked flame of an underground lake of molten lava... something immensely powerful struggling to get out...

...just like Karen.

LITO VALLS

by Amy Roberts

Rafael "Lito" Valls' face splits into a grin of delight as he considers the question of what make St. Johnians unique.

"It used to be that a taxi driver on St. Thomas would take you wherever you wanted to go, likewise on St. Croix. But not so on St. John. They'd tell you point blank, 'I'm going fishing!'"

He punctuates this statement with his characteristic staccato laugh, but then quickly resumes the more serious demeanor of the scholar.

"I've always maintained that the people of St. John are more independent than the people of the other two islands," says Valls, who as a historian, writer, teacher, and librarian, has given considerable thought to the matter.

"I think it came about because after the slavery system was abolished, most of the people of St. Croix continued to live in a state of 'serfdom.' They were bonded to a given plantation, and they weren't allowed to exchange places of work or employer except for one day of the year — the first of October. So they remained in a form of bondage under the plantation system.

"On St. Thomas, the people were organized around the port. Most people lived in town, working as coal carriers, or porters, or what have you. But on St. John, most of the people started acquiring land. Whether they bought it, or it was given to them by the former owners, or they squatted on it, they worked their own land, and they did their own thing. If they wanted to go fishing, they did. If they wanted to make charcoal or baskets, they did."

It is this spirit of independence, among other qualities, that made Valls, a native Crucian, choose St. John as his adopted home back in 1972.

Actually, destiny may have had as much to do with it, for it was almost Lito's fate to be born on St. John. When Lito's mother was pregnant with him back in 1927, Abram Smith, her "adoptive" father, offered to give the family Caneel Bay Plantation, which he owned. Smith felt the place was going to ruin, and he wanted the family to live on the property and maintain it. But Lito's father was adamantly against it. "I'm not going with my family in that bush!" he declared.

At that time, St John was said to be "behin-gad-face" — "behind God's face," Lito explains, meaning remote, inaccessible, and backwards. So the family picked up and moved from St. Thomas to a three-story colonial home, which better suited their lifestyle, across from Government House in Christiansted.

Smith hung on to Caneel Bay until 1936, when he sold it to the West Indian Company for the handsome sum of $10,000. Now, of course, the luxury resort that was developed there is worth millions. Lito just chuckles as he thinks about what might have been his. "My adoptive grandfather thought he'd won the grand prize — that was a lot of money in 1936."

As you may have surmised, Lito was born into the upper echelons of island society. Daniel Valls, his father, was raised in Ponce, Puerto Rico, the center of the sugar industry where most of that island's wealth was concentrated. After finishing a university course as a teacher, Daniel was sent to St. Thomas, along with many other educators from Puerto Rico and the mainland, to help

"Americanize" Virgin Islands schools in the early 1920's. (This was shortly after the territory's transfer from Denmark.) Daniel became principal of Charlotte Amalie High School, the island's first secondary school.

Lito's mother, Maria, was also from Puerto Rico, but she spent much of her early life on St. Thomas. When she was nine years old, she was sent to St. Thomas for the summer to visit with friends of her father. Although she was unable to speak English and was homesick and miserable, an outbreak of bubonic plague in Puerto Rico prevented her return.

Eventually, she did go back to Puerto Rico, only to find that she was now homesick for St. Thomas. She wound up living with the family of Abram Smith, the wealthy St. Thomas businessman, landowner, and chairman of the Colonial Council, who essentially adopted her.

Daniel and Maria were married in 1922 and their first three children were born on St. Thomas. When he decided to leave his position at Charlotte Amalie High School (and rejected the offer of Caneel Bay), Daniel took over as principal for Christiansted High School. But his interest in education soon waned and he went into business for himself; Daniel opened a grocery store — actually it was more of an emporium — selling everything from cod fish to Nash automobiles.

In spite of the fact that he had been the principal of a public school, Daniel insisted that his own children attend parochial and private schools. Lito, his brothers Daniel Jr. and Quintin, and sisters Florence and Lina, were all packed off to exclusive academies in Puerto Rico.

Lito attended Colegio Ponceno in Ponce, a school with a reputation for snobbery which was probably well deserved, as it produced at least two of Puerto Rico's governors. "It was a bit of culture shock for me because my mother was very democratic," Lito admits.

"One day when I was living with my father's sister in Ponce, I was sitting in the enclosed patio near the servants' quarters, chatting to the maids and the cook. My aunt came to the window and said she wanted a word with me," said Lito, his voice taking on the hushed tone of a boy attempting an act of contrition.

"I sat down, and she sat down across from me in her rocking chair and composed herself before saying anything. Then she said, "I don't know what kind of household your mother ran in St. Croix but in this house, one does not chat with the servants!" He bursts into laughter at the recollection.

Lito never was comfortable with his status as one of the elite, and although he mixes well with the guests at Government House, he's more likely to be found in the evening with a cold beer in his hand, chatting with friends near the ferry dock in Cruz Bay.

His discomfort with prestige stems from his school days in Ponce, when students at the Colegio Ponceno were still brought to school by horse and carriage. (This was during World War II, when gas was being rationed.) Lito and his classmates, who wore military uniforms to school, were taunted by the town kids as "blanquito" — meaning "very white" or "upper class." To this day, he still has an aversion to uniforms.

Although he developed a distaste for elitism, Lito took the best of what his upbringing had to offer — education — and he has used it well. He attended college at the University of Dayton in Ohio, which despite its secular name, was a Catholic institution. He graduated with a major in psychology and a minor in history in 1949. One year later, he obtained his master's in public administration at the University of Puerto Rico.

When Lito returned to St. Croix after completing his studies, he was at a loss as to what to do. He was toying with the idea of getting another master's in industrial psychology when Pearl B. Larsen, then the director of the Department of Education on St. Croix, convinced him to take a summer teaching job.

Lito's students were not your ordinary high school pupils. They were all returning veterans from WW II, taking advantage of the G.I. Bill to get high school diplomas and go on to college. Lito was by far the youngest person in the classroom. Louis Brown (who later became Commissioner of Labor) was one of Lito's students, and he took pity on his nervous young teacher.

"Louis said, 'May I be excused?'" Lito recalls with a laugh. "He went across the street where there was little rum shop, and bought a bottle of rum, six cans of Coca Cola, ice and cups. Then he distributed them to everybody in the class, and after that we all relaxed."

Although he never expected to do so, Lito ended up teaching Spanish and geometry at Christiansted High School (now Elena Christian Jr. High) for several years. Once again, destiny seemed to have something to do with his decision. When he opened the teacher's textbook for Spanish class, he found his father's name inscribed in it from the days when he had been an educator.

Over the years, Lito influenced a number of young people who later went on to positions of authority. He taught (Governor) Juan Luis and (Judge) Eileen Petersen. When Lito left the classroom to work in the public libraries in 1953 his proteges included (attorney) Winston Hodge and (Hess executive) Alex Moorhead.

It was during those years that Lito met (Delegate-to-Congress) Ron deLugo and became vigorously involved in politics. His friendship with deLugo seems to be another example of the role of fate in his life. Lito's mother had been taken to visit Ron's grandfather, Antonio deLugo y Suarez, so she could speak Spanish when she was living on St. Thomas as a child. The families had been friends for years, but curiously, Lito and Ron had never met.

Ron, Lito, and Mooie (a.k.a. Theovald Moorehead, see related story) began to organize the Democratic Party in the late 1950's to challenge the powerful reigning Unity Party. Ron, who ran for senator-at-large from St. Croix in 1956, could not speak Spanish with any fluency; this was a problem on an island with 40% Hispanic population. Lito campaigned for him in Spanish, and deLugo won.

As Ron ascended the political ladder, he was elected "Washington Representative," a position which Lito describes as "a glorified lobbyist." DeLugo became good friends with John F. Kennedy. (Lito has pictures of the two of them with their feet up on the desk in Sen. Kennedy's office.) From Washington, deLugo lobbied for the establishment of the position of delegate-to-Congress. When the new position was created in 1972, deLugo ran for it and won; despite sporadic challenges, he's managed to hang onto that job ever since.

Ron tried to entice Lito into a career in politics, but ultimately he wasn't interested. As a political plum, Lito was appointed assistant commissioner of the Department of Tourism in 1969, but he quit after a year and went back to the libraries of St. Croix. When Ron won the delegate's seat in 1972, he once again tried to get Lito involved by offering him a job as his assistant.

But Lito had other plans in 1972. "I was starting to get fidgety about St. Croix," Lito explains. "They had introduced large industry there, and the infrastructure wasn't ready for it. A lot of immigrants had moved in from all over, and the crime rate was going up. After a few little incidents in town, I spoke to Mrs. Enid Baa, who headed the libraries on all three islands, and asked her if there were any openings on St. John. Ron offered me three times the salary, but I told him, 'No! I'm going to St. John before St. Croix explodes.'"

Lito's instincts were, unfortunately, right on target. Just as he landed the job on St. John, St. Croix erupted with violence. Eight people were gunned down on a golf course in what's now known as the Fountain Valley Massacre. "I picked up the phone and called Ron," Lito says, "and as soon as he heard my voice he yelled, 'Shut up!'"

Lito came to work in the library of the Julius E. Sprauve School, (which also then served as the public library) in what is now the police station. Inspired by Florence Lewisohn's book *St. Croix Under Seven Flags*, Lito started to develop a passion for local history, as well as a growing interest in West Indian dialects.

"George Seaman had put together a little dictionary of island creole. Linguistics were not his field — he was a naturalist — and he did it as a lark," Lito explains. "But I was fascinated with it. I began making notes to send to him whenever he published a second edition. One day Ron was here visiting and we were sitting in my studio; he was looking at my thousands of note cards. He looked up at me and said, 'Are you really going to send this thing to George Seaman? You must be some kind of ass! You've got a book here!' That's when I realized I had written a book without really trying."

Lito thought about publishing the book but decided that the high printing costs made the whole project too complicated. Then fate once again stepped in. It was 1982, and Lito had just left the library to work as a historical interpreter for the Virgin Islands National Park.

"I didn't realize it, but I was working my way to a heart attack," says Lito matter-of-factly. "It was a very frightening thing, but once you get over it, you realize that you have to do something — all those years, and nothing to show for it! The heart attack was very instrumental in getting me going in my own writing. It gave me the impetus to take those notes for a dictionary and put it into a book."

Thus Lito's first book, *What a Pistarckle — A Dictionary of Virgin Islands English Creole*, was born. The book was first published by Doris Jadan (see related story) as a fundraiser for her Environmental Studies Scholarship Program. Valls was on a roll. He soon published *Old Time Sayin's — Proverbs of the West Indies*, and *The Supplement to What a Pistarckle!*

Continuing his interest in folklore, Lito's next book was a collection of traditional West Indian riddles entitled *Riddle Me One, Riddle Me Two*, which Lito swears "was written by my alter-ego, a fellow named Jan Kallaloo." The next book (co-authored with Ruth Low) was also written "by accident." "Ruth and I were doing research for the museum at the Battery, and we soon realized we had enough for a book." *St. John Backtime*, a priceless collection of old journals, photos, and narratives, now stands as one of the best available sources on the history of St. John.

Lito has two other books to his credit, *The St. John Historical Coloring Book* for children, and the more scholarly *Brother Cornelius and Thomas de Malleville*. (The latter is about an enlightened stonemason, a slave who worked his way to freedom and built the original Emmaus Church in Coral Bay, and the governor-general at that time. Unfortunately, the book is out of print.)

As an employee of the National Park, Lito now shares his knowledge about St. John history with locals and visitors. And if you want to get a true sense of the island, its traditions, and the families that have made St. John what it is today, you've got to take the Historic Tour that Lito leads for the Park.

Here's where you get all those juicy tidbits of information of who's really who on St. John. As you wend your way from Cinnamon Bay to the East End, you learn about William Henry Marsh (born in 1832), whose father was chief justice on Tortola.

"He had family here — he was related to the Hill family who owned Cinnamon Bay," Lito explains. "They were all wealthy people, and he inherited money from them. William Henry Marsh had managed the estate at Reef Bay for a wealthy German landowner, and eventually he bought it and a lot of other land.

"The story is he got a girl — who was his housekeeper in Reef Bay — pregnant. He went around trying to court one of the white girls, but none of the planters' daughters would marry him after the scandal. Eventually, he married the girl, Lucretia Titley, and took her to live in the Great House in Reef Bay. When W.H. Marsh died in 1909, he was the largest landowner on the island. All the Marshes, still major landowners on the islands, are their descendants."

Lito also tells us that the Boynes and the Sewers (whose last name, incidentally, is derived from "de la Soeur") all descended from white Haitian planters who were kicked out of Haiti during the revolution in 1792. The governor of the Virgin Islands, not knowing what to do with the emigres, gave them land on the East End of St. John.

The Penns also have a long tradition in the islands. They descended from a nephew of William Penn who settled on Tortola in the 1750's. ("He apparently got into some kind of trouble, and the better part of valor told him to take a ship out of Boston to the West Indies," Lito explains). The Penns, like the Lettsomes, Callwoods, and Thorntons of Tortola, had at one time been Quakers.

Lito can trace the Sprauves back to Dutch Reform Church records from the 1740's, and associate the Samuel family to Wickham Cay on Tortola. He can trace the Mooreheads' arrival as part of a wave of immigration from Sint Maarten in the 1860's.

Lito has always had a love of U.S. and European history, so he gleefully traces the histories of the families to their European ancestors. But he's also very aware of the traditions and contributions brought by the Africans to St. John.

He makes it clear to his listeners that the Africans were not one homogeneous group that can be lumped together as a single culture. The Africans who were brought to the Virgin Islands as slaves were as culturally diverse as the people who now make up the islands.

That is one of the reasons that St. John had a full-scale slave rebellion in 1733. Some of the slaves here were former leaders of warrior tribes, and many had been slaveholders themselves. They absolutely preferred death to bondage and mounted a rebellion that took the combined forces of the French, the British, and the Danes to quell.

With his knowledge of history, Lito is able to clarify some of the myths regarding St. John. He'll tell you, for instance, that legend has it that the rebel slaves leaped from Mary Point rather than surrender. That's never been documented, Lito says, but it is true that some number of slaves did commit suicide at Ram Head.

Lito also likes to clear up some modern misconceptions about St. John's development.

"In the 1930's, ten families from St. Thomas, and one from St. John (the Marshes) owned 90% of the land on St. John. They were hanging on to it for speculative purposes, and were only too happy to unload it to Rockefeller at the fair market value. Those people who owned little plots, of two or three acres, still have them," he maintains.

"The census will also show that per capita, more St. Johnians own their own homes than anywhere in the Virgin Islands. And more St. Johnians own homes than before the park was established. So this fallacy of the Park buying up land so that no one can build is a bunch of bullshit!"

Lito's passion to set the record straight makes him momentarily lapse into the vernacular. Normally, he's very disturbed by profanity, and its growing popularity is a cause of concern to Lito. "You don't hear so much profanity on St. Croix, and you never used to on St. John." He recalls a saying from his youth: "St. Croix is the lady, St. Thomas is the whore, and St. John is the Virgin."

St. John has a tradition that is different from the other islands, Lito says. "You never used to see a man on St. Croix or St. Thomas holding a baby, but here you did. And you never saw a man hanging out clothes as you did here. I attribute that to the fact that there was traditionally more family life on St. John. You know, in the 1930's, Governor Paul M. Pearson visited the Moravian Church and congratulated the people of St. John for having the highest rate of legitimate children throughout the territory!"

St. John has changed, but not all that much, Lito says, and aside from the congestion in Cruz Bay, he's happy here. Although he has talked about moving away to a quieter island, Lito really never plans to leave St. John. He owns land on which he's trying to build his dream house — a little native West Indian cottage. "I've attempted three times and failed, but I'm trying again," he says gamely.

In the meantime, he lives in a prefab in the National Park housing compound which he almost manages to disguise as his fantasy cottage. Lush tropical plants surround his home in the otherwise barren development. If you want to reach him, you have to follow local custom and call "Inside!" through the open door because he refuses to have a telephone. It's just one of those things that he's stubborn about.

"I admit to being obstinate, indeed, willful. I don't give in, and I will hold a grudge for life," says Lito, who declares that he's no candidate for sainthood.

But, he says philosophically, there's a positive aspect to that quality, which he defines as his most salient good point. "I don't give up," he says. "I suppose I get this from my two favorite people in history: Mother Theresa, who when asked about the futility of her efforts to combat poverty and pestilence and dirt and disease, answered quite succinctly, 'We're not called upon to be successful but to be faithful,' and Winston Churchill, who delivered the shortest speech of his life to the students of his old prep school 'Whatever you do in life, never, never, never give up!'"

Ernest

by Cap'n Fatty Goodlander

Ten kids is a lot of kids, no matter how you count 'em. That's how many children Ernest (Sr.) and Mariel Matthias had. Ten mouths to feed. Father Ernest worked 30 years for the St. John Department of Public Works. He helped build most of the roads on St. John. Mother Mariel wore a number of hats besides her most important jobs as housewife and mother; she currently works in Senator Almando "Rocky" Liburd's office.

Ernest (Sr.) and Mariel still live on the beach at John's Folly on the East End of St. John, just as they did in the mid-1960s. Back then, like many of the people of St. John — while they were wealthy in a number of important ways — they didn't have a lot of cash money. They had the house, the land, family, friends and a job — but not much else.

Not with ten mouths to feed.

One of those mouths was Ernest Jr. Even as a baby, he was a bundle of energy. He even *crawled* fast. He was a speedy kid; always in motion. Restless. Raring to go. Eager.

Everyone in the Matthias family had their daily chores. Work came first; then play. Their family house was as much farm as residence. The kids tended to chickens, goats, pigs, ducks, geese — even the dogs and cats had to be looked after. That's not even mentioning the daily work in the garden, carrying water, taking out the garbage, and all the rest of the tasks of island living back in the '60s.

Everyone had to do their fair share. There was no getting around it. Young Ernest literally ran through his. "Bing, bang, boom!" — and he was done. Then he'd lope off to the beach to do a few high-spirited speed runs — just to burn off some more of his seemingly boundless energy.

"We didn't have many toys back then," Ernest said in a recent interview. "So all my toys were sticks. Each of my sticks represented a certain piece of heavy equipment — a dump truck, backhoe, or bulldozer — and I'd race up and down the beach driving them, backing them, turning them... making their machine sounds... tooting their horns... shifting their gears..."

Ernest was, and still is, intrigued by heavy equipment. Some of the most vivid memories as a youth are of his father skippering a piece of heavy equipment while road-building. "Each evening, I'd leave my equipment — my sticks — in a certain way. Nobody was allowed to mess with them, and nobody did."

Ernest would usually jog the three miles over to the basket ball court in Coral Bay each day — and play some pick up basketball, or just shoot some baskets. (Ernest's first trip off St. John/St. Thomas was to St. Croix to play high school basketball. It was an eye opener. "The thing I remember most was the size of those St. Croix guys," says Ernest with a rueful smile. "They seemed like giants compared with the guys I played ball with back in Coral Bay.")

Growing up, Ernest and his pals freely roamed the East End of St. John. They traveled mostly by foot. There were not many organized community events back in those days, and so they made their own fun as best as they were able.

Ernest liked to repair and ride bicycles too. Somebody would give him an old bike frame, and he'd barter for some used wheel rims, a seat, a pair of handlebars...

"We just would make do with whatever we had. Most kids had hand-me-down bikes made up of different parts gathered over the years. They worked — most of the time, anyway."

Ernest and his buddies would burn up a lot of energy, and would resupply themselves along the way. "We'd eat genips, locust, soursop, sugar apples, coconuts — you name it! We didn't think anything of living off the land. We'd just look around, and grab what was handy when we got hungry. Everybody did. And everything we did was a race, a contest between us. We had a lot of fun."

"Back in those days, my cousin David Hendricks was the fastest coconut tree climber on the entire island. He could climb up a palm tree in nothing flat. For years, I tried to beat him, and never could. Man, he was fast!"

As much as Ernest loved the shore, he also developed a love for the sea at an early age. "I loved playing on the beach and swimming. We'd go skin diving, and hunt for lobster, conch, and whelk. We'd go spear-fishing. Somedays we practically lived in the water."

Ernest's grandfather, Lancelot Wiltshire, had an old wooden skiff pulled up on the beach near their house. Ernest accompanied his grandfather aboard the boat whenever he could, and learned how to handle a boat at a young age.

"Once, me and some friends, we 'borrowed' my grandfather's boat — and ended up capsizing it. Man, I got in plenty trouble — *plenty* trouble — over that one."

When the sea was up — and the waves big — Ernest would swim out between the breakers, and body surf to shore. He and his friends would also build small boats from discarded materials, and have daring contests of seamanship in them.

"We'd build what we called 'bateau' boats. We'd take a piece of discarded "galvanized" (corrugated tin roofing material) and make a boat out of it. We'd use wooden two-by-fours or driftwood for the transom. We'd collect some used nails, which we'd straighten for the job..."

They'd take a rectangular piece of the tin, and cut a triangular-shaped chunk out of one end so that when they folded it — the shape of the bow of the boat emerged as if by magic.

The tin boats were about eight or nine feet long, usually. The biggest problem was keeping them watertight — but, as usual, Ernest and friends had a practical solution based on the materials at hand.

"Even back then, there was pollution in the water. Somewhere in the Atlantic there would be an oil spill — and the result would be soft tar balls — large clumps of sticky globs of solidified oil — washing ashore on the beach at John's Folly.

"This stuff — depending on what we mixed with it — was perfect for waterproofing the bows and transoms of our little boats. It would even stop little pinhole leaks — which were a real problem since we were using used galvanized in salt water..."

On calm days they'd paddle their boats all over the place. One of their favorite tricks was getting in and out of the little tipsy craft in deep water without sinking it. It looked easy, but was anything but.

Of course, this difficult trick had to be learned the hard way. Since the boats were metal, they sank like stones if swamped. If you lost your boat in water too deep to dive it back up, you had to build another. "It took me a couple of boats, but I finally got the hang of it," said Ernest.

In heavy surf, they played a far more dangerous game. "First, we'd see if we could manage to row out through the surf without swamping. If we made it beyond the breakers, we'd wait for a lull, and surf back into the beach. Sometimes we'd ride a real big one back into the beach. This was tough on the boats, but the speed was thrilling."

Ernest first attended pre-school on the East End. He doesn't remember much about those days, but he recalls that the teachers allowed him to skip kindergarten, and go straight into first grade at the Guy Benjamin School in Coral Bay.

"Miss Eudora Marsh was the principal then. She owned the Sputnik bar too. Coral Bay was quiet. Everyone knew everyone; many were related by family. For instance, my cousin Lewis Lomax is the son of our current Administrator, Bill Lomax. Bill

Lomax's wife — Lewis's mother — is my Aunt Zenny."

"The older kids from Cruz Bay used to tease us 'country' kids on the East End by calling us 'Coral Bay moose!'"

"Yvonne Tharpes taught pre-school back then in John's Folly. She later became a policewomen, and now is a lawyer — I believe."

"Later, Mr. Prince was one of my teachers. He taught crafts. He was a wonderful instructor, but very strict. If you misbehaved with Mr. Prince, you paid the price right then and there. There was no arguing with Mr. Prince.... yeow!"

It was elementary school which first exposed Ernest to organized sports. "I liked track and field. Even though I wasn't really tall enough, I enjoyed playing basketball. I enjoyed most all of the school sports..."

When it was announced that a major marathon was coming to St. John, Ernest immediately went into training for the event. "The second year they ran it, there were about 100 entrants. I was the first guy from St. John to finish. It took me 55 minutes to run from Coral Bay to Cruz Bay. I came in fourth. Right behind me was Alberto Samuels. We felt pretty good about our showing, considering how many good runners there were in the field..."

After Guy Benjamin School, Ernest rode the bus into Cruz Bay to attend Julius E. Sprauve School. Then a few years later, he rode the ferry to St. Thomas to attend Eudora Kean High School.

During his high school years, Ernest worked summers. "I did lots of construction work and road building jobs. I learned to drive most heavy equipment."

After high school, Ernest went to Washington, D.C. for almost a year of vocational training in heavy equipment. "I didn't like Washington," said Ernest. "Too cold. And I missed St. John. But, looking back on it — I'm glad I went. I think sometimes you have to leave a place to realize how nice it is.

"As far as living in the United States — well, I think I learned a lot in those eight or nine months I was gone. The world is a big place. There's lots of stuff going on. The whole experience opened my eyes in a number of ways."

It was also during this time when Ernest got back involved with boats and the local marine community. "I used to hang out around

Coral Bay Marine, and visit with Tom Gerker. Everyone was real nice to me, and I was soon helping people out with their boats.

"The first time I raced was with Tom Gerker. It was during one of the Thanksgiving Regattas sponsored by the Coral Bay Yacht Club. We sailed on a big fast red boat named *Sirocco*. I loved it. Yacht racing was sort of confusing at first, but I gradually made sense out of it."

The following year, Ernest raced with Vicky Rogers and Thatcher Lord aboard their John Alden-designed 33 foot sloop *Bounty* — and became one of their regular racing crew. The more Ernest learned about boats, the more he wanted to know. Gradually over the years, he became a much-sought-after crew member.

In 1991, he raced aboard the 50 foot ketch *Perseverance* owned by Larry and Lee Best of Scituate, Massachusetts. At one point — this was again during the Coral Bay Thanksgiving Regatta — one of the two jib sheets came loose from a high-cut headsail.

This was a serious problem. The wind was really piping up, and the race was a tight one. In order for the vessel to tack to windward, the racing crew would have to drop the headsail, reattach the jib sheet, rehoist the sail, and then square away again. This would take a lot of time — and cost them a number of places in the race.

Instead, Ernest put the bitter end of the unattached jib sheet in his mouth — and then lifted himself off the deck with his bare hands by holding on to the remaining jib sheet. Slowly, hand-over-hand-over-hand, he moved out over the water. Everyone on board held their breath — thrilled at what he was attempting to do, horrified that he would fall into the sea.

Finally, he arrived at the clew of the straining sail. By this point, Ernest was dangling far to leeward of the boat, suspended over the large heaving waves as the boat surged ahead under full racing sail.

The boat's motion through the seas made it difficult to stand up on deck — let alone hang on to a rope. It was obvious to everyone aboard that Ernest was going to have to work fast.

Ernest took a deep breath — and suddenly he was dangling by only one arm! With his free hand, he threaded the end of the dacron sheet through grommet in the clew of the sail, and then calmly tied a perfect bowline knot *with only one hand*!

As Ernest slid back towards the deck, the crew of the ketch *Perseverance* broke into spontaneous applause — and Ernest's accomplishment immediately became part of the yacht racing folklore of the Virgin Islands.

As his love of sailing and racing blossomed — and his acceptance by the marine community became universal — Ernest decided to get serious about his seamanship.

"I went to St. Thomas, and signed up for a crash course to get my US Coast Guard captain's license," said Ernest. "After studying hard, and carefully documenting my sea time — I took the test and passed."

He was soon working as skipper of the dive and sightseeing boat named *Ocean Diver* (now *Sadie Sea*) which operated out of Cruz Bay. "I enjoyed being on the boat, and out on the water," said Ernest. "And I enjoyed the people. I get along OK with all types of folks, and running a charter boat — well, you meet a lot of different kinds of people."

About this same time, Ernest fell in love with another competitive sport — a sport about as far away from sailboat racing as imaginable.

That sport was... bobsledding.

"A fellow from St. Thomas named Danny Burgner was interested in getting a VI bobsled team together to compete in the Olympics. He mentioned to Cid Hamling at Connections that he was looking for a strong fellow to be a pusher — and she mentioned my name. The next thing I knew I was in Calgary, Canada, getting my bobsledding license! This was in 1988..."

Soon Ernest was jetting off to Switzerland, France, Canada, or Austria to train as a "pusher" of bobsleds — and having his picture taken with movie and sports stars from around the world.

"It was really wild," recalled Ernest, as if he still can't quite believe that it all really happened. "Once I was at this big fancy party, and across the room this guy is yelling, 'Ernest! You have to come train with us!' and, like, it's Prince Albert of Monaco..."

As interesting as the social part of bobsledding was to a young Virgin Islander, it was the actual sport which enthralled Ernest.

"Yeah, well, I guess I already told you I like to go fast. Speed is... I love speed. There's nothing quite like the feeling of going 70 or 80 miles an hours on a bobsled. Now *that's* fast!"

The 1992 Winter Olympics turned out to be one of the highlights of Ernest's life — and it also contained some of the lowest moments.

"Carrying the VI flag into the Olympic Village during the opening ceremonies — I just can't explain how it felt. My hands were sweating. I was so scared of making a mistake before all those TV cameras — with all the entire world watching. The sound of the giant crowd — the huge noise it made — was deafening as we came marching in. The lights were so bright. A million things seemed to be happening at once."

The two weeks Ernest lived in the Olympic village was like a dream. "Everyone was so nice — so friendly. You know — you hear a lot about the comradery of sportsmen — but it's really true. Everyone was... like a family in the village. Nobody was better than anyone else. There was a lot of emotion, a lot of energy, a lot of intense friendships..."

"And the food! Every time you turned around, there was another buffet waiting — just brimming with all the healthy food you could possibly eat! Each evening there were parties, meetings, ceremonies, and sports demonstrations..."

Cynthia Smith, Ernest's girlfriend, accompanied Ernest to the Olympics. She's originally from Tennessee, and runs the snorkel tours at Trunk Bay in the National Park.

"One night, Cynthia and I went to a party with about 3,000 drunken Germans. They had a wild rock band playing, and we told everyone Cynthia was a famous County and Western singer from the United States. A few minutes later, there was Cynthia up on the stage, crooning C&W western into the microphone while everyone in the audience stomped and cheered."

But there were low moments, too.

"Going into the last race, we had a chance to come in maybe 22 out of 30 — and beat Jamaica, Monaco, etc. But, for a variety of reasons, our team captain elected not to race. I was... disappointed..."

When Ernest speaks of learning he wasn't going to get that final opportunity to reach for glory — to get his final speed fix of the Olympics — his voice shakes. It is obvious that he would have gladly crawled the bobsled back up the track in his teeth for the chance.

"But that's the way things go sometimes. I'm very grateful to have had the opportunity to participate. I would have liked to do better than last place, but..." he says with a twinkle in his eye, "there's always next time..."

At the time of this writing, Ernest is again concentrating on watersports. In fact, his hobby of sailing and his profession have come together quite nicely.

"I'm running the watersports concession out at Maho Bay," Ernest says. "We rent sunfish, windsurfers, kayaks, etc. I do a little teaching. It's fun."

Ernest is always into something new. He loves change, welcomes a challenge. He's worked as a mechanic on the local ferry boats, as a landscaper for the National Park — even operated his own dump truck company for awhile.

Ernest's enthusiasm for life — and his love of his fellow man from every stripe of life — is plain for all to see.

"I'm pretty easy going, I guess," he says. "Nothing really bothers me. I like people. Sometimes I get taken advantage of 'cause I'm so easy going — but not too often. I stay out of trouble; I'm not interested in drugs. Someday I'd like to own my own home, maybe even a boat...

"Sure, St. John is changing fast — but it's still a great place to live. There's plenty of opportunity — plenty of work, if you're willing. Some people say it's getting too crowded, but if the tourists suddenly stopped coming — where would we be? A lot of us would be out of a job."

What's the future hold for Ernest? "I don't know," he readily admits. "I'm making pretty good money right now, but I'm always thinking about tomorrow. I've had some interesting job offers lately — but I don't want to change just for change's sake, I want to move *up* if I'm going to move at all."

"And, of course, I still like to go fast," admits Ernest. "Whether on a bike, sailboard, or bobsled — I *still* love that sensation of flat-out speed. It's a thrill I still haven't outgrown.

"Also, sometime in the future, I'd like to work with the local kids here on St. John. I want to teach them to swim, to windsurf, and to sail. Somebody has to teach them how important it is to preserve our natural environment — for everyone's sake. Especially theirs."

It's typical of Ernest to want to give back to the St. John community some of the warm support it has given to him over the years.

To raise money for his Olympic quest, some friends of Ernest's organized a huge fundraiser at the Inn at Tamarind Court. It was an all day affair, and hundreds of people participated. Thousands of dollars were raised, and the good vibes were so thick you practically had to swim through them to get to the bar.

During the event, at various times a multitude of community leaders said complimentary things about Ernest — but it was near the end when one of the emcees of the event took to the stage and said, "By sending Ernest to the Olympics, we aren't just sending another athlete to another international sporting event — we're also sending a goodwill ambassador from the island of St. John out into the world.

"The person we send should represent the very best we have to offer as a society. It should be a person that we all respect, admire, and love. It should also be a person who brings us together as a people — a special person that we citizens of St. John are especially proud of..."

The crowd was already cheering, 'Ernest! Ernest! Ernest!' as the MC continued, "And how many of you here today think that special man — that special ambassador — should be Ernest Matthias..?"

The resulting applause was thunderous; nearly drowning out cries of "Ernest! Ernest! Ernest!"

Of course, Ernest has never forgotten that day. He may have been 'bahn here' on St. John by random chance, but he lives here by heart-felt choice. He's proud of his birthplace, proud of his home. And it, too, is proud of him.

All and all, not bad for a kid who was famous for running up and down the beach at John's Folly with a handful of sticks imitating the sounds of heavy equipment.

Annabelle Apple

by

Lynda Lohr

Annabelle Apple dispenses kind words, advice and feisty opinions along with the daily newspaper from her post behind the counter at Fred's.

"She's outspoken and she lets the chips fall where they may," said her long-time friend Thelma Dalmida, also a woman not afraid to take a stand.

And from Lee Hansen, another granddam with firm convictions, "She was spitfire then and she's a spitfire now. She's not afraid to state her opinions even in the face of adversity."

According to Doris Jadan, she never adjusted to the idea of West

Indian leisure — the sense that nothing ever changes.

Jadan said she is respected by nearly everybody in this small community of about 4,000.

"She obviously cares about what's going on," said Jadan.

Miss Annabelle, as she's affectionately known by one and all, touches more lives than just about anyone else in St. John.

In fact, many of her customers reflect the diversity of people who live in St. John — and are as colorful as Miss Annabelle.

And many are equally outspoken. Morning discussions in the store often involve several people interjecting conflicting opinions.

"Throw all the senators out," said one customer as a steady stream of customers plunks down their 50 cents for the morning newspaper.

Hardly a soul fails to pass by Fred's for their newspaper. And those who don't appear as expected are likely to get a phone call asking if they're sick.

"Oh, you're going to work late today," is a familiar remark from Miss Annabelle, who notices everything.

She lets one man know that his mother went to St. Thomas on the 9 a.m. boat, passes on documents left by a friend to another, and loans out the phone to someone needing to make a call.

"Why not, it's a small thing," she said, chuckling at the thought of charging for such services.

She suggests Visine to customer Irv Rubin and sends him off to the drug store for help.

"She's full of gloom and doom this morning," joked Rubin, as he and Miss Annabelle exchange gibes.

She tells plantman Andy Rutnik that she's been having better luck with her plants.

And after a bit of pleasantry with Oswin Sewer, she asks the age of the baby in his arms.

When she hears 22 months, she shakes her graying head.

"It doesn't seem possible," said Miss Annabelle, who's watched more babies than you can count grow up to have babies of their own.

She's been selling newspapers and various and sundry items for all of her 28 years here — first at the Apothecary, which later became V.I. Aids, and after that store closed two years ago, at

Fred's.

"She belonged to a very special group — the working women. She wasn't monied like most of the whites who came years ago," recalled Hansen.

She remembered her as a hardworking woman who was always cheerful.

And according to Jadan, she's been known to take in a stray donkey or two.

Miss Annabelle, now 68, arrived on vacation from St. Petersburg, Fla. with her boyfriend and two daughters — Debbie, now in her 30's, and Connie, in her 40's — in tow. (Her son Walter stay behind with her former husband.)

After two weeks at Huldah Sewer's Guest House, the boyfriend returned to Florida.

"No big thing, it happens all the time," said Miss Annabelle, laughing a bit at the long-ago memory.

"And I never left the islands except to go to Puerto Rico," she recalled, wondering why anyone would want to go elsewhere.

In fact, she's so delighted with life in St. John that she thinks moving here was the best thing that ever happened to her.

She was born in Greensburg, Pennsylvania to a coal miner and his wife and spent years in a coal mining town so small it had no name.

Her brood has grown to include four grandchildren and three great-grandchildren, one of whom — 12-year-old Ayala — helps her fetch the newspapers from the ferry boat each morning.

"He's almost as tall as I am, but I can still knock him in the head," says Miss Annabelle.

She's not shy about dispensing verbal blows to those whose actions or opinions seem out of kilter.

Local politicians frequently get the barb as she learns of their antics on Addie Ottley's morning show.

"What's wrong with Virdin Brown, letting Bryan run wild like that," ranted Miss Annabelle, speaking about two members of the 19th Legislature.

Of course she stood in line to vote this past election day.

"It's an honor and a privilege to vote," said Miss Annabelle, recalling that she couldn't wait to register to vote.

She's seen it all during her years in St. John. She's watched St. John grow from a sleeping town with a smattering of tourists who fit into the local scene to a hustling mini-metropolis complete with crime.

"There's nothing wrong here except the dope situation," said Miss Annabelle, who watches the town's shadier characters amble past the door.

She attributes the drug-related crime problems to a breakdown in community values.

"Years ago the cops would take kids home to their parents, but not now," she said.

A casual conversation in the store which unexpectedly developed racial overtones really gets her goat.

"Don't tell me somebody took something away from you," she said, advocating that those who continue to complain that the whites who've come to St. John have succeeded where they have not should put their shoulder to the wheel and get to work.

She said that when down-islanders first came to St. John in the 1960's and 70's they worked hard, bought 10 cement blocks each payday, and soon built their houses.

"They didn't spend their money on drink," she recalled.

No stranger to hard work, Miss Annabelle is behind Fred's counter — always wearing a colorful shift — six days a week.

Ever the optimist, she can't come up with anything bad to say about her life even when pressed.

Retirement is some distant day in the future because she has to pay for the Bethany House that Hurricane Hugo blew away in 1989.

Miss Annabelle lived her first 20 years here in a small wooden house on Pocketmoney Hill with gravity-fed water from a rainbarrel.

"She loves her breeze and her view, but she's lived in tough conditions. She's made do," observed Jadan.

And what does Miss Annabelle do for fun?

"Gardening," said Miss Annabelle, who always keeps an array of colorful hibiscus blooms near the counter at Fred's.

She's proud of the fact that her green thumb has grown to the point where she can "stick a piece of wood in the ground and make it bloom."

Discoursing on gardening problems, she does complain that the hot sun and lack of water cut the odds for success.

When the last newspaper is sold, the final "how ya doing" said, and all the hibiscuses watered, what does Miss Annabelle do?

"Go home, have a few beers, watch TV and fall asleep," she joked.

Lynda Lohr was born in South River, New Jersey and moved to St. John in 1984. She is a full-time professional journalist and has worked for such publications as the VI Daily News, the Associated Press, Pride Magazine, and the St. Croix Avis.

Sis Frank

by

Susan Barry

Three decades ago, Cruz Bay looked and felt like an idealized tropical island — an island that existed, for many, only in the imagination.

Approaching the beach-fringed harbor, a visitor saw one or two boats anchored, island residents swimming, and the children diving off the dock or fishing with hand-held lines. A few Tortola sloops eased by, graceful and silent.

There were no structures near the dock, though Miss Elaine Sprauve might be taking her rest on the front porch of her yellow house by the sea. The house is still there and so is Miss Elaine, but the palm trees and sea grape have obscured the view to the uninitiated eye.

It was a quiet, peaceful, friendly place where the rare arrival of rowboats and dinghies were greeted by all present with both curiosity and a smile. There was one telephone on the island, with five extensions, one of which was on the dock. But with few vehicles, folks could be heard talking for blocks around. The sounds were of the sea, the palm trees rustling in the "trades," the laughter of children and the soft easy voices of residents — at home — on their island.

The Cruz Bay Park was filled with large shade trees and a few benches. The Customs House, built on stilts, was to the left. The largest structure was Meada's Inn — a one story, West Indian design with lots of gingerbread. Miss Meada's peacocks wandered at leisure, screeching as the spirit moved them. Miss Myra (Keating Smith) and Miss Meada could be heard passing the time.

The men were 'limin' around Mooie's, maybe shooting a little pool, taking it easy. After all, it was Sunday.

And on that Sunday a young woman from upstate New York named Ruth Pflanz set foot on St. John for the first time. She went on to make significant contributions to the island she chose to call home, became Mrs. Carl Frank and today is known as 'Sis.'

"Well, I came here thirty-three years ago in 1959. Can you believe it? I was sent here by an old friend who owned Lavender Hill, and Lavender Hill in those days was not what it is now. It was a main house and a guest house that hadn't been finished. And one day he said, 'Gee, would you go down there and find out where all my money's going?'

"I said, 'Sure, why not?' My mother and I had lived in Haiti when I was thirteen, and I never forgot the smell of the charcoal and the beautiful mountains. My father traveled in the Caribbean a great deal and I just think it was kismet that I came to live here.

"I arrived on a Sunday, as I remember, and I looked over from Red Hook while I was waiting for the one ferry that was supposed to come, and there was a double rainbow over the island and I just, to this day, feel that was a special omen. It was to be that I would come here.

"One of my jobs was to work for The Corporation, which was

formed by Ron Morrisette, Sr., who now is gone, Elaine Sprauve, Mooie (Theovald Moorehead), Albert Sewer and many other wonderful St. Johnians and Victor Bornn, Edie Bornn's (Attorney Edith Bornn) father over on St. Thomas.

"The Corporation was formed for the purpose of selling stock and buying ferry boats. It really was an attempt to establish the first tours for St. John and a regularly operating ferry boat company. Loredon (Loredon Boynes, Sr.) was a boat captain and so was Victor Sewer.

"The Corporation eventually failed, but it was an attempt to do something. I was their helping hand, I guess you might say.

"I would go down to the dock and Loredon Boynes and Victor Sewer and Rodney Varlack and all the others who worked for The Corporation would have our daily pow-wows about what to do, and what not to do. Of course, they teased me constantly.

"One day Victor said to me, 'Now, go over to the West Indian Company and get a silencer for the *St. John.*'"

"I though, 'Gee, I wonder was a silencer is?' Well, I guess I could figure that out. It's a muffler — and sure enough they had it and I got it and brought it back and Victor praised me, for once, as I remember.

"Of course, we're great friends now. All those men, putting up with a greenhorn from the States — really, they were wonderful to me.

"Another part of my job was to mix the punch for the tour. Now the tour was only — if we had a tour — once a week, and I mixed the punch at six in the morning. Then the tour director probably wouldn't show up, so I would have to go. In those days we went around into Charlotte Amalie Harbor and, of course, I was sea sick by the time I came back.

"But I kept it up because I believed in The Corporation, and if we had maybe 25 people, we thought it was a big day — I mean a Big Day. It was really thrilling. I'd have to go rushing over to Miss Meada, who made the sandwiches, and say, 'Make more, there are more people.'

"Communication between the two islands was not the greatest, so people would just show up and I'd have to make do.

"But living in those days, everyone knew everyone else and

everyone spoke to everyone else on the island. There were so few people here you just lived everybody's lives.

"Did I tell you how many people lived here? There were 900. And among the 900 there were only 80 continentals and half the time they didn't speak to each other, for some crazy reason.

"But you know, I don't remember in those days that people tried to tell us what to do. I think we all kind of grew up together. I mean, if we felt that something different should be done on the dock, we'd sit down and talk about it peacefully, and it would be done.

"I think now that it's kind of a mistake for people, in my way of thinking, to come here and say, 'Well, back in Philadelphia we didn't do that.' They don't know how long it's taken us to come to where we are. This is why [local] people have a little resentment toward people who come and say, 'Hey, why are you doing it that way?' And I look back and I think, 'Oh, if you only knew the agonies we went through to get to where we are.'

"We all — and I think of Victor, Loredon, Rodney, and Elaine Sprauve as being the oldest living people left from The Corporation — we've softened. I don't go to the [public] meetings any more because I can't stand to hear people yell at each other.

"Back then we did have many challenges and the food was one of them. We had a lovely little stores — Miss Alma and Austin Smith had one, and Luis Encarcion had another one. I think that was about all we had for food — and mostly canned things.

"I always remember a wonderful story about Austin Smith. He suddenly got TIDE, big packages of TIDE detergent and I said, 'Oh Austin, that's marvelous. Of course, they were all sold in about two days, and I said, 'Gee, aren't you going to get any more, and he said, 'No, they sell too fast.'

"We would order our meat from the Nevada Meat Market on Columbus Avenue in New York. It would be sent down on a container ship. Sometimes no one would tell us when it was scheduled to arrive. We'd have to run down to the dock to rescue it from melting. If people didn't come for their meat, we'd take it home and put it in our freezer.

"But you can see it was a magical life then. We all had such fun. We all went to Eric's old Hilltop, where the St. John School of the

Arts is now, and we danced. We had a lovely, lovely life and there was no crime. Well, this is true all over the world. Everything has changed.

"But I look at St. John now and I think, 'I'm so fortunate to have been here all these years, and to have been accepted, and to have been a kind of late-coming pioneer.'

"There was no one to take care of homes when I came. In fact, there were no [rental] homes. As they were built, people would say, 'Sis, would you take care of our house? Would you rent it and so forth?' and I said, 'Sure.'

"Suddenly I had fourteen houses, after they were all built, and it just kind of developed itself and it had no name. Now you have to give everything a name. It was the beginnings of Holiday Homes.

"Eventually, in 1960, my husband to be, Carl Frank (who was in radio and television in New York and had been coming here for years) heard from Duke and Kay Ellington (who owned Gallows Point) that there was a girl on the island who had never married. So he sent me a postcard and said, 'Wait for me'.

"Well — I kind of did. Oh, it's a wonderful story. We were married, it took him a year to convince me. He became the tour director for The Corporation, and, naturally, he had a walkie-talkie radio. As they would pull out of the harbor, he would talk to me all the way around into Charlotte Amalie. Marvelous salesman, you can imagine that.

"We were married in 1962 and Carl added the business aspect of what became Holiday Homes. We became the first realtors on the island, and he also created St. John Insurance Agency.

"Carl would walk around the street with all the bills, and maybe ten of them in his hand, and people would pay him on the street. Well, eventually, it got so big we had to have files, and I don't know whether we both liked the idea of the business getting so large. At first we ran the business out of our home and eventually we had about 32 houses that we took care of.

"The Mom and Pop [operation] got to be a little out of hand and then we had to have an office in Cruz Bay, and I think we both kind of resented that.

"Carl became ill and he passed away in '72, and I took in Peter

Griffith as a partner. Peter had come here with his family in the '60s and when we became partners, I began to realize that the island was changing, and I really didn't enjoy the real estate business as much as I did before.

"And, as you know — a wonderful thing dropped in my lap.

"One day I went by Julius Sprauve School and I heard the steel band that had just been formed practicing and I thought, 'Gee, they sound pretty good.' So I dropped in, and the director Rudy Wells and two of the children came up to me and said, 'Mrs. Frank, if you like the band so much, we're beginning to have engagements, and we can't keep track of them. Would you be our business manager?'

"I thought, 'Business manager of a steel band? I don't know about that.' But of course, I did, and it was wonderful.

"That year they (Steel Unlimited I) went to the Rose Bowl, and I'll never forget the lecture Rudy gave to them. I thought, 'Wow, he really has captured these kids. He's got them in his hand, and this whole thing is fascinating.'

"The next thing I knew we went to Florida and we recorded twice. We've sold those records for all these years, 18 or 20 years. We've sent children to college, bought books for them, whatever they needed. They each got a monetary stipend in the beginning, and that band was out of this world.

"We traveled. Some went to Denmark, Washington, New York and again to Miami. We went to Disney World — in those days it was just beginning. That was in 1972 and the band performed until 1976 when Rudy went off to the Berkeley College of Music and received two degrees in music, with honors.

"Then he came back and I said, 'Okay, let's have another band' and he said, 'No, let's expand it. Let's teach band and piano and all those other good things. And I thought, 'Wait a minute!'

"He said, 'Let's have an arts school.'

"Rodney Varlack, Rudy, and I met on my porch on a Sunday morning and we laid out the plans and went from there. The only thing is that it took us ten years, from 1980 to 1990, to build the building and never again would I rely on volunteerism. It's, you know, one person doesn't show up so nobody can do anything.

"Glen Speer, who designed this beautiful building, was out of this world. He would appear and work on his own for three and four hours. There are many people in this town who have given and given, either materials, or labor or both.

"During that ten years Elroy Sprauve, who was our vice-president, and I ran piano lessons and we taught them at the Lutheran Church. We also had art classes at the Church, so we kept up what we were trying to do.

"Rudy and I tried to get the band together. We got new pans from Trinidad but it just didn't work. Juel Rhymer was kind enough to allow me to store the pans at the Youth Multi-Purpose Center. But if you don't have your own building, it is very difficult, very difficult. So we gave that up.

"By the spring of 1990 we were able to start dance classes at the St. John School of the Arts. We started ballet, Isadora Duncan dance, modern dance, and we started another steel band — Steel Unlimited II.

"That summer we had a program for children 8,9,and 10 years old. These were little children who had never held a stick; maybe some of them had seen a pan before. Rudy worked his magic, as he's been doing for forty years, in pan. The next thing I knew they could play — a little better and then a little better.

"In the fall of 1991 we gave our first concert and over 250 people came to see. Well, I must share something with you. Terry Chinnery and Orville Brown, who were old players of Steel Unlimited I, stood with me, and the three of us had tears running down our faces. Really, it was too much.

"Both Terry and Orville have gone on to apply what they had learned in Steel Unlimited I — discipline and self-esteem. They run another program that I was involved with, Young Athletes in Action, and they do such a marvelous job.

"Steel Unlimited II went on to perform thirty-eight times between November of 1991 and this past July, raising money for our trip to Disney World in Miami. Rudy feels, and he's quite right, that the children must have something to aim for. You can't just rehearse every day and not go someplace. It opens their eyes and is really quite exciting.

"For several of the children the trip was their first trip off the island. From all reports — and I got reports twice a day, practically — the children behaved beautifully, and people were fascinated by them because they were so young. They range in age from 9 to 18 now, most of them from 9 to 12, boys and girls. There are 26 in all.

"They performed first at Bayside Market in Miami. Then they went to Criteria Studios, where the first band recorded, and made a tape which we now have on sale. Then they went to Cape Canaveral, spent five hours there, on to Disney World, and stayed at Fort Wilderness and had a ball there.

"They gave three performances at the American Dream Stage, Epcot Center and the Magic Kingdom, Tomorrowland. The men who are in charge there had no idea what they were getting. They called to tell me that they had no idea that they were such beautiful children and that they played so well.

"It did something for the children. When I returned in September I could see that they'd grown, not just a year, but they'd grown in every possible way.

"So you can see how much I love what I do. The School is my whole life now. I'm here — all day."

Susan Barry has worked locally for such newspapers as the Tradewinds, the VI Business Journal, and the Nautical Scene. A graduate of the University of Oregon, she currently hosts the talk show Talkabout St. John *on Radio One WVWI.*

John Anderson

by
Ruth Low

When John Anderson, thirty-one year old Harvard graduate, arrived on St. John at sunset in February 1936 with his artist wife, Adrienne Adams, there was nothing to foretell how profoundly this island would affect their lives.

No trumpets sounded. No banners appeared in the sky to predict that this slender, wiry man, whose deep-set blue eyes held poetry and a glint of humor, would one day rediscover and enrich a neglected period of St. John's history.

Over the next forty years, through intensive and infinitely painstaking scholarly research during his free time, John Anderson accumulated a multitude of facts to replace the incomplete information and myths that had surrounded St. John's bloody six month slave rebellion of 1733. His book, a detailed no-holds-barred narrative, *Night of the Silent Drums* was published in 1975.

In an introductory note, Anderson explained how he made use of his research. "The events in this book took place, as nearly as I have been able to determine to my satisfaction, as described here, and all of the names are the names of real people who existed in the times and places in which they appear. The fiction lies in the links that are missing in the source material that I studied; and these I have filled in, from hints in the material, with my imagination."

The Andersons had chosen St. John for their delayed honeymoon after reading Desmond Holdridge's captivating *Escape to the West Indies*. For a place to stay, they sought out Paul Boulon, Sr., in Puerto Rico, who is identified as the owner of a camp at Trunk Bay where the Holdridges had lived.

As they stepped ashore on St. John from the weekly mailboat, they asked how to get to Trunk Bay. The administrator arranged for their luggage and supplies to be taken by rowboat but they decided to walk. "Trunk Bay is about four-and-a-half miles, you'll know it because it's the first sign of human life you'll see."

One of the first things they did after settling in was to charter the *Speed* to go to Tortola. "She was an interesting cargo sloop belonging to Captain Williams," recalled Anderson. "As we sailed between Mary Point and Whistling Cay, Captain William told us the legend of the slaves throwing themselves into the sea and the rocks turning blood red."

"This made such an impression on me that I went back later, many times, and stood there looking down, spellbound, into the fearful whirlpool. That was until I learned that it never happened. In all my research I have never found even a hint that such a thing occurred there.

"But it is such a dramatic spot that one is ready to believe. And I was a passionate believer. What I didn't know until twenty years later was that almost every unsuccessful slave rebellion in the western hemisphere has such a legend of people holding hands and leaping to their deaths from a precipice.

"As soon as we got back to the States, I went straight to the New York Public Library to see what I could find out about the rebellion. Dr. Waldemar Westergaard's *The Danish West Indies under Company Rule* was the best thing there. His section on the rebellion didn't satisfy me at all, but I made a copy of his bibliography. At that stage, I expected to get most of my information from printed sources. From there on, I just followed my nose.

"At the Library of Congress in Washington I discovered that the transcribed copies of the Danish records had innumerable inaccuracies," said Anderson. "Because of my familiarity with the islands I was able to spot many of them. It was these inadequate transcripts that convinced me that I would have to go to Denmark.

"Then, when I got a chance, I went to California to look at the Governor Gardelin order and letter books in the Bancroft Collection at Berkeley. There they were, the original handwritten orders issued throughout the rebellion. They were, of course, in Danish, Dutch, and later, French.

"A Danish newspaper man offered to translate the Danish parts for five dollars a page. I had already started to learn Modern Danish, so I decided to do it myself. It was this Gardelin material that gave me my start in reading 18th century handwritten Danish and Dutch. By the time I had mastered the 277 photostat pages of the order book, working with 18th century dictionaries, I had become pretty good at reading Old Danish. My greatest cross throughout the entire research was the difficulty deciphering the many individual handwritings in gothic script."

"On my first trip to Denmark in 1955-56 I spent the winter in the State Archives. It was one of the coldest winters in years, and the government buildings were the only warm places in the country. I practically lived there. Up in a great barn of a room on the top floor were mountains of documents that no one had classified. The archivists became my personal friends and let me dig to my heart's content. I found what I wanted, and had it microfilmed.

"Before I left, I had consulted with the Danish Museum at Kronberg Castle, Elsinore, the Royal Library, The Danish Naval Museum, the Library of the University of Copenhagen, the State Church Archives, the Danish State Museum Archives, the King's private library, and the private archives of families with West Indian connections. I came away with enough material to keep me busy for many years. Whenever I had some spare time I would work with my microfilm viewer. I had a ball, just loved it."

The Anderson's returned to St. John frequently. At one time they managed the Helen Payne cottages, and one season they lived on St. Thomas. In 1950 they bought their land above Cruz Bay, hacked their way to it with a machete, and, in 1959, started building.

Anderson alternated his years of intermittent research, including two more trips to Denmark and side trips to Norway and England, with tenacious explorations searching out the locations of the rebellion in St. John's deep bush. In the beginning, he tramped alone, hacking his way through long forgotten trails. Later, at the insistence of his wife Adrienne Adams (known as Dean), he went with friends Dib Woodside and Steve Edwards.

"When I would stand on a spot where some of these things happened — my hair would stand on end. With a forty year saturation you get pretty deep inside yourself. Deduction has been an important tool for me. If you know what they did, their background, the circumstances and the actual places, you can pretty much imagine the details.

"Every person in the book is an actual person. Their names turn up again and again in official documents, land records, vital statistics, and tax records. The ships I write about are actual ships that arrived on those actual dates. The weather, with the droughts, the storms and the critical phases of the moon occur on exactly the dates these things happened.

"I have lived so long in 18th century St. John during the months between November 1733 and August 1734, that some of the people in the book are almost more real to me than some of my long-time friends.

"There are probably about 300 characters who come and go during the course of the action. Dr. Cornelius Bodger, who was spared by the rebels to care for their wounded, is my leading figure. All the important things, the philosophical things are expressed by him. He usually says what I feel.

"There were probably fewer than 100 genuine rebels. A great many of them were enslaved against their will by the rebel leaders. Most of the slaves, but not all by any means, originated around the area which is now Ghana.

"The most important breakthroughs in the book, I feel, are the relationships between the rebels themselves, and also their movements about the island. Until I got deep into the source material I didn't know the locations of most of the historic spots where the action took place. These came as a surprise.

"I had originally planned to write a rather romantic historical novel. But as the details emerged from my research year after year, they were so intensely human, so totally fascinating that I determined that they must stand on their own, without artificial plotting.

"What had given me the confidence that I could get away with straight fact treated as fiction was Truman Capote's 'In Cold Blood'. That book made it possible for me to write a book which could be published as a novel, and yet still tell the truth.

"I wrote the initial chapter quite early. But from there on, I soaked myself in an ever-growing pool of fascinating material. I didn't start writing in earnest until the accumulation of facts and ideas caused labor pains to begin.

"Then, working seven days a week, I wrote the book in two short vacation winters here on St. John and three weeks in New Jersey. Actually, the book almost wrote itself."

"When I was writing the book here on St. John, I would get up about daylight, grab my satchel, and walk up Centerline Road to Steve and Nancy Edwards house above Pastory. They were in the States, and the solitude was perfect for me. I'd cook up an enormous breakfast of cereal, bacon, eggs, toast — the works. Then I'd start writing and keep going without a break until mid-afternoon.

"If I know what the next sentence is going to be when I stop work in the afternoon, I can start right off in the morning. If not, I write letters to get started. Writing is the most difficult of all professions. The self-discipline is tremendous.

"I divided the book into five sections. In the first and second I tell what an average day was like on St. John in 1733, and show the gradual development of the will to rebel. 'The Abyss', the third section, is the opening day of the rebellion. 'A Writhing of Worms,' the fourth, is to me the most interesting and the most human: it shows they were just people in a sort of deadlock situation where no one could see which way things would go. The last, 'Spider in the Horn', which was my original title, shows how the rebellion finally came to an end. It was never really put down. In a curious way, it just ended.

"By the time I got to the last part, I had nearly a thousand pages each of typescript and carbon copies. Like an idiot I had the two piles stacked near me, each anchored with a rock — same as I'd been doing all winter there on the Winter's gallery without a problem. Then suddenly a tremendous gust of wind from the south knocked the rocks off and scattered pages all over the side of the mountain.

"Nearly two thousand pages dispersed over ten acres of bush, kasha, catch-and-keep — some even in the tops of trees. Rounding them up took several days. Luckily, it didn't rain at night and the wind prevented dew. Eventually, I was able to recover all but about ten pages. I still work outside on St. John, but now I use really big rocks.

"The reason my manuscript was so long was that I couldn't bear to leave anything out. I think I really wrote the first draft for St. Johnians, to share everything I had learned. Over the years so many pieces of information just dribbled in from all sources, things that provided an astonishing number of very plain hints as to the action.

"There are points of conflict with other accounts of the rebellion. Though some writers have depended heavily on Christian Martfeldt's report, I have not used it. As a historian, he let his imagination run too free. Also, I interpret various clues differently from some of the other writers.

"Official records on individual slaves included their classification as household, artisan, or field workers, and in many cases, the circumstances of their capture in Africa, what ship they came over on, and at what slave auction they were sold.

"Until the King of Denmark took over the Danish West Indies for the Crown in 1754, the islands were the private property of the Danish West India and Guinea Company. Additional records of individuals are the lists of rebel and loyal slaves submitted by planters to the company compensation through unnatural loss of slaves. Rebels would be recognized during skirmishes and reported.

"Though I was able to find quite a lot of material on the slaves, I was able to use only about a tenth of it. Much of this information came from G.C.A. Oldendrop's 1777 book *Geschichte der Mission der Evangelischen Bruder auf der Carabischen Inseln St. Thomas, St. Croix, und St. Jan.* It is a history of the Moravian missions published at Barby on St. Thomas, now known as Nisky. As far as I know, it's never been translated into English.

Oldendorp was a missionary who apparently talked endlessly to the newly arrived Africans. He asked some very inquisitive questions, somehow got away with it, and found out some very informative things — some wonderful, and some preposterous.

Of course, some who read the manuscript wanted me to sex it up, and hoke it up. Ironically, that's what I'd set out to do in the first place. But, as it turned, out the exception to the 'hoke it up' school of thought was Charles Scribner, Jr., and my editor under him, Laurie Graham. I had already cut the original manuscript by about a quarter, but the whole thing seemed so interesting I just couldn't give up any more. It really took a second pair of eyes. Working with Laurie, we cut out another quarter. All of which came out of my bleeding flesh.

"We had to cut two whole sequences, whole families, whole chapters; she was a cold-blooded murderess! But I have the greatest respect for her as an editor, and know very well that it is a far better book because of her. When I go to see her, sometimes I wear a black armband as a silent reminder, but I love her dearly.

"My only real problem was the sales department. They rejected my introduction and bibliography. They insisted it would hurt the sales of the book as a novel. They did, however, allow me a glossary of unfamiliar terms, and I think they are letting me have a brief explanatory note. I tell you, salesmen rule the world.

"One thing I'm very concerned about here on St. John is that many people expect the book will be a history. It is not; it is a work of fiction. I wish people wouldn't call me an historian. I am not," he said emphatically.

"It was clear to me early on that I couldn't get enough details of the rebellion to make a continuous story. But I wanted to know everything I could, to base it on fact as far as that is possible. There are no records of the intimate human elements of the conflict. No survivors to tell the story. All that perished with them."

Then he added, "Slavery is not the villain of the book. It is human nature. Man's inhumanity. One thing that bothers me somewhat is the conviction that this book should have been written by a St. Johnian from the authentically black point of view. However, no one can say that I didn't give them plenty of time."

-==-==-==-

The above material was based on an interview with John Anderson in the spring of 1975, shortly before *The Night of the Silent Drums* was published.

In the early 80's, the Andersons left St. John and went to live in San Marcos, Texas. It was there that, after a long illness, John Anderson died on April 24, 1993. He was 88 years old.

His book, out-of-print for a number of years, has recently been reissued in a handsome edition with more-or-less contemporary illustrations by MAPes MONDe of St. Thomas.

A token of Anderson's deep affection for the people of St. John was his assignment of all future royalties to the St. John School for the Arts.

Ruth Low divides her time between Massachusetts and St. John. She is a freelance journalist with an avid interest in St. John history. She co-authored the wonderful book St. John Backtime (ISBN 0-961-4355) with Lito Valls. It is a rich collection of highly interesting and entertaining stories about old St. John.

Elvis Yearwood: Island Entrepreneur

by
Susan Barry

St. John is not immune to the social ills plaguing the rest of the world, nor is it exempt from the idea that greater career opportunities might exist elsewhere for its residents. Many young people leave the island to "make it". Some return, some do not.

Because of this, there is a persistent outcry for successful role models on the island.

One of the most successful, dynamic, and innovative businessmen currently living on St. John is Elvis Yearwood. He's a Kittitian by birth and a St. Johnian by choice. He's also the owner of Paradise Gas, Paradise Laundromat, Paradise Water, Paradise Health Club and the soon-to-open Subway Sandwich franchise.

How did this entrepreneurial effervescence come to be? Just ask

Elvis.

"I came to St. Thomas when I was about three-years-old. I attended first the Ulla Muller School, and then the Washington School, and I finally graduated from Charlotte Amalie High School in 1978.

"Most of the time in high school I played music. I played the trombone. I spent so much time playing music, I almost didn't get *out* of high school! At the time, I also studied air-conditioning and refrigeration. So, by trade, I'm an air-conditioning and refrigeration repairman.

"That's what brought me to St. John in 1978 or 79. I was the only refrigeration mechanic on the island for awhile. I worked at Caneel Bay and I took care of all the air conditioning and refrigeration needs on St. John before I became a police officer.

"I was a police officer for close to ten years. I was involved in the K-9 corps for about six of those years. I had a K-9 named Brownie, and we made headlines almost every week. We recovered a lot of stolen property. We arrested a lot of people for drugs and burglary.

"Brownie was from St. Thomas. He was just a great dog. When we gave K-9 demonstrations at schools, I'd send him around the classroom. He'd play with the kids real nice. And then I would give him a command, and he'd change in a split second. He could be real aggressive — you couldn't even touch him.

"He was a Doberman Pincher, and he was feared by everyone. He could be mean when he had to be mean, and he could be friendly when he had to be friendly. To me, that's the kind of dog which should be in the K-9 corps. Since I resigned, St. John has not had another K-9 officer. People miss this kind of service. People always like to say, 'Send the dogs up and let them track the scent and maybe you can try something or do something.'

"When the K-9 comes on the scene and he tracks through the bush — even if he doesn't find anything — you feel like somebody did something to help.

"I don't know about people in the States, but I know that some West Indian people would rather be shot than have a dog bite them up. They're very particular about dogs. If for some reason they know the officer on the scene they might say, 'You can't shoot me, you can't shoot me.' But they can never say to the dog, 'You can't bite me' — because that's always a possibility, even if it happened by accident.

"I read there was going to be a new K-9 officer on St. John, but I haven't caught up with her yet. I'm going to tell her that as long as she is over here and as long as I can be of any help to her, you know, lay her tracks for her, agitate her dog, whatever it takes to get a real fine police dog back into St. John, I will be of help.

"After I left the police force I bought the propane gas company (Paradise Gas). We handle all the bars, restaurants, schools, campgrounds, hotels, and homes on St. John.

"The following year, well, I can't say I did so well. The last time I had an interview, I told them that I cared more about my customer's satisfaction than I cared about their money. That was a mistake. Everybody say — 'Oh, he have so much money, he don't care about it!' So now I gotta be real careful when I'm giving these interviews...

"But I did all right. The following year (1989) I opened the laundromat one month before Hugo hit. Two days after Hugo I had current (power) back on. I had people coming from St. Thomas to the laundromat. At the same time, I had a good supply of gas on the island, so I didn't need to get any gas. So we did pretty well.

"The following year I did the health club. It's about 1,000 square feet. We have quite a large selection of equipment. We have a Stairmaster, Universal (Gym), free weights, and a leg press machine. It's air-conditioned and we have qualified attendants on hand.

"Also, we have this guy from the States, Alexis, who does personal training. He's good and he gets you going.

"The following year I did Paradise Water Manufacturing. We bottle drinking water. I must say it is the finest bottled water anyone has ever tasted. I did a lot of research and spent a lot of money trying to get the quality right. I'm selling almost as much water as gas.

"I also invested in water coolers which I rent to stores, offices and businesses. I have a man who does nothing but deliver water all day long.

"As I was telling you earlier, somebody was telling me I was better to be born lucky than be born rich. I was lucky — not rich at all, oh man, not rich! When I started out I hardly had anything. I was just lucky that every business I started was able to hold its own right away.

"And I will tell you I am blessed with the ability to pick good employees. The people who work with me — we get along like brothers and sisters. We work hard together. I'm there all the time, and I treat people fairly. I don't lie to them. I don't try to say one thing and mean something else. We get along really good.

"When you are starting a business you have to look at the needs of the community. For example, when you want to reach for something and can't find it on St. John and you say, 'Gee, I'm going to have to go all the way to St. Thomas for that....' and then your brain start tickin' and you say, 'Whoa, maybe I should really check this out. Why do we have to go to St. Thomas to buy spare parts and small appliances? Why can't I do it here?'"

Good advice from a man who knows. There is a certain irony in the fact that Elvis Yearwood was the recipient of a Small Business Administration Award, yet he has never had a loan from that organization.

"That is correct.I have never had a small business loan. What happened, I would call Mr. Battiste for directions. I would call him and I would say, 'You know, Battiste, I have an idea about X,Y and Z.'"

"And he would say, 'It sounds good, you know, Elvis, but be careful. Look at this, look at that.' He was very helpful advising me yet I never had a loan from them. But you know, I think I'm on my way to them with this Subway thing, because this is more than I can handle.

"I bought a Subway franchise last year but I couldn't find a suitable location in Cruz Bay. So I found an empty lot and now I'm having to put up a whole big building just to open up a Subway shop. It's a heavy investment which I didn't anticipate.

"But in any business — location, location, location. If it's not right, don't do it. I'm telling you... if it's not right, don't do it. I have to say it twice because it's a fact. If you are not in the right location, forget it. People don't like to even walk up steps — unless it's something like the gas company where they have no choice."

With all the responsibility for running five businesses — and counting — does Elvis have time for anything else?

"Yes, I'm a member of the Private Industry Council and also a member of the St. John Singers. My mom named me Elvis! She knew right away what was going to happen. I'm a tenor and sing with John Cahill. We put a lot of work into our singing."

By example, Elvis Yearwood, the entrepreneur, is a role model. He started with a dream and has built up his businesses by hard work. What advice would he give to young people who would like to try their luck?

"Well, I don't know. If you want to get into business, you have to do a lot of research first. You have to have the dream — you have to have the want — you have to have the ability to work hard. Even though I have a lot of employees and all these businesses — I still work seven days a week. I work long hours — eight, nine o'clock at night I'm still at it.

"But it all starts out with a thought. First, you think about what you'd like to do. Then you look in the books, you look in the catalogues. You think about your community. What does it need?

"If you live in a community like St. John for five, ten, or fifteen years, you got to know its needs, you got to know its wants. So you jump right in and work hard. You don't stop, you don't stop. Borrow some money from your sister or your brother, and don't stop. Because the time you stop — the next day might be the big day.

"I'm always busy. And people say to me, 'Elvis, what gonna happen when you get married?' Notice I'm telling you that I'm not married yet? That's another thing. You got to know about your personal life. If you're going to get involved in business, you got to get somebody who understands what it calls for. If you have a question in your mind whether that person is going to understand it or not — then it's best you stay by yourself.

"I'm just waiting for my Subway shop to open because it's going to be a big, big hit in St. John. I haven't slept a night. As a matter of fact — I think it's going to be bigger than any of my other businesses."

Spoken like a true entrepreneur.

Cid

by

Cap'n Fatty Goodlander

Cid Hamling of "Connections" has always been a good girl. She went to college. She studied hard. Eventually, she got a couple of degrees. Thus armed, she left her family home in Atlanta, and set off in search of High Adventure. She had few specific goals; and only two things she was determined to always avoid. "I didn't want to be a waitress or a secretary," she said. "No way! I wasn't gonna hustle tables nor jab at a typewriter. Ever!"

She was born in 1948 in Minneapolis, Minnesota. Within a month of her birth, her parents, Coe and Betty Hamling, moved the family to Atlanta, Georgia.

Cid was the middle child of five kids. It was a close-knit family of high-achievers. There was a lot of love, and there was some pressure too. She lived somewhat in the shadow of her two older siblings, while her younger siblings were forced to live within hers. Even as a child, she was expected to realize that every action had a consequence — that you had to live with the results of your actions. The values of hard work, education, and community service were continuously drilled into them.

"My grandfather died when my father was a baby. He was raised by his mother in a sod house in South Dakota. She was a country school teacher, and they were poor. His mother stressed to him that the key to a full life was education. After high school, he hitch-hiked to a college, and told them he'd do anything to attend. Despite his lack of money, they accepted him. He eventually graduated from Hamlinge College (no relationship) in St. Paul, Minnesota, which is where he met my mother."

Once his family was settled in Atlanta, Cid's father went to work for the Robin Hood Flour company. A hard working man, he quickly moved up the corporate ladder. Soon he went in business for himself — creatively financing furniture store inventories.

In some respects, it was the most American of families — the embodiment of the American Dream. "Raising five college-bound children in the 1950s was no small achievement," said Cid. "My family has always been very important to me. We're still very close. Their support — their uncritical love and acceptance — has always been something I can depend on. I can always turn to them. They've always been there for me."

If all this sounds a little like the old TV show "Leave It To Beaver" — it should. There's a weird connection. "While my father was in college, the Wrigley Spearmint Gum Company sponsored a nation-wide talent search among college students. He ended up representing Minnesota, and was sent to Hollywood for a screen test. The competition consisted of three parts: dancing, singing, and acting. My father did fairly well, but was beaten by a young fellow named Hugh Beaumont — who became, of course, Leave-It-To-Beaver's father."

Despite the fact that Cid spent nearly her entire childhood in Atlanta, she never really felt she was a child of the South. "We were different because my parents were Northerners. I always felt a little bit like an outsider."

There were other ways in which Cid's family was different. "My parents were members of the Unitarian Church. Religion and spirituality are still very important to them. This was in a town where you were either Baptist or Methodist — period. Once the church held one of its annual conventions in Atlanta, and my parents threw a big 'welcome' party to kick things off. A couple of the church members attending the party happened to be black. The following evening, someone burnt a cross in our front yard."

Cid's first major adult decision in life turned out to be a disaster. "I was so nervous that I wouldn't be able to get into a good college — that I decided to go to the first one that accepted me. That happened to be an all-girls Methodist College in Macon, Georgia. My parents thought it was a bad choice — but since two of my favorite girlfriends were going, and it was in the same town as my boyfriend's college — I insisted. They finally said OK. About a week into the new school year, I realized it was a mistake. Now it was their turn to insist that, mistake or not, I had to complete the entire year. I did, just barely. And learned the hard way that you have to live with the full consequences of your decisions. That's life. That's what being an adult is all about."

The following year, Cid attended Hamlinge College in St. Paul. She'd never been north, and didn't know a single solitary soul in the entire school. Once again, her accent was wrong. Once again, she was different.

Yet, despite the difficulties of the geographical transition, she accomplished it quickly. "It was in St. Paul that I really learned to depend on myself. If college taught me anything, it taught me that I could do almost anything I set out to do — if I worked at it. I graduated in 1970 with double majors in Sociology and Special Education."

She taught in Minnesota for awhile, but quickly decided that the weather was just too cold for comfortable living. She returned to Atlanta, and began teaching kids with special needs. "Because of a recent court decision, this was the first year many of these kids attended school. Many of them hadn't been tested properly. Some of the students who were considered to have various degrees of retardation just had behavioral problems. One poor kid was perfectly fine — just deaf. They were all just lumped together. It was a very stressful year."

She went back to college, and obtained a master's degree in counseling psychology. She soon was working as Executive Director of the Department of Mental Health in Anderson County, South Carolina.

"About this time, I married. My husband was soon hired as the City Manager of Clemson, South Carolina. It was a small, tightly-knit college town. I was never really happy there. We were viewed as the 'perfect yuppie couple'. We had a boat, and we flew airplanes... but something was missing."

She got more and more into her work. "There was all this Federal money available to help people with special needs — but much of it just wasn't being used. When the Federal Government had asked Anderson County — the fifth largest in South Carolina — how many of its citizens could be classified as retarded, it replied 'none'!"

"So the challenge was to build a complete social framework to assist these people — many of whom were getting help for the first time. Some of the situations were unbelievable — one women was literally chained in the front yard while her parents went to work because they just couldn't figure out what else to do with her."

"My department had little funding, so I harnessed all the idealistic college students in the area. They had tremendous energy and dedication. Everyone said that it couldn't be done, but within a relatively short span of time we brought some order to the chaos. We wrote a lot of grants, and helped get a lot of social programs off the ground. Suddenly, the people who needed the most help were actually starting to get it."

"This taught me that — despite the nay-sayers and the odds stacked against you — important things can be accomplished if you stick with it. Consistency is important. In a sense, all of my life has revolved around some aspect of social work. In this case there were people who needed and deserved help — and my team enabled them to get it. Sure, there were times when it was extremely frustrating, but there were also plenty of times when it was very very satisfying."

Cid was growing increasingly tired of both Clemson and her marriage — when the Department of Health, Education, and Housing (HEW) made her an offer she could not refuse. It sent her back to college — all expenses paid — to study family counseling.

"I never looked back. I got my master's in social work from the University of Georgia in January of 1980."

After working in the field the following year, Cid decided to take a break "...for two or three months."

She studied to be a clown, and worked as a mime in Boston. She sold BONG-BONGs on the streets of Cambridge — those crazy wobbly glittery styrofoam balls on the springs which clamp to your head.

Suddenly, life seemed to be offering her a number of exotic adventures. Her new-found freedom seemed almost intoxicating. She was loosening up, going for it, winging it, loving it, tasting it — jumping at the chances.

Cid was suddenly making up for lost time.

A friend invited her to go sailing, and she soon found herself working as a cook/deckhand on a private yacht. Job followed job, and she worked on a number of private and charterboats in Florida and the East Coast.

She loved the sailing life; its unexpected freedoms, the lively people, the little mysteries of each foreign port.

Such a romantic life.

But, of course, one must make a decent living. Life is a serious business. The future must be planned for.

Cid jumped ship in Cruz Bay, St John.

And there you have the two main ingredients of Cid's personality in a nutshell — the hopelessly romantic and the imminently practical. The starry-eyed idealist and the hard-nosed business woman. The Dreamer and the Doer. Ms. Ying & Yang — all rolled up into one six foot female package of brains, brawn, and beauty.

So, anyway, where were we? Ah, yes... Cid jumping ship in St. John. She loved the island from the very first moment she stepped ashore, and her love has continued to grow. (Her devotion to St. John is steadfast, like a naturalized citizen's love of America. She equates St. John with her personal rebirth. Don't knock St. John around Cid, ever.)

She immediately fell in with the In Crowd: local economic Guru Forrest Fisher started bending her ear about how much opportunity there was in the V.I. for an imaginatively creative businesswoman.

"St. John just seemed special back then. The Back Yard, Mongoose, and Mugsy's were filled with interesting characters. It seemed everyone I met was an artist. The streets were perfectly safe; everyone left the keys and their stuff in the car. And the music was everywhere! I danced and danced and danced!"

Idleness isn't Cid's strong suit. She's a very active person. She immediately sought gainful employment, and found it.

She worked hard as a waitress at Cafe St. John (ex-Cruz Quarters, now JJ's) for a few years to save up enough money to open Connections... which quickly grew into the largest answering and secretarial service in the entire Virgins.

"Yes," Cid says with a rueful smile, "Life can be kinda weird at times."

The reasons for the rapid growth of Connections was, at least in part, because of Cid's background as a social worker. "The main part of a social workers job is putting people in touch with the resources they need. In many ways, a business person operates they same way — they see a gap and fill it."

"People on St. John needed an address, an answering service, a place to make long distance calls. I gave it to them. That operation then grew to include photocopying, secretarial, and notary services. The charterboats came to me, and soon I was acting as their booking agent."

Only Cid could have pulled it off. She enjoys making new things happen — has an enormous amount of personal energy. Her powers of mental focus are awesome; as is her ability to handle a myriad of incoming detail without mishap.

In 1988 Cid was named "Entrepreneur of the Year" by the VI Business Journal. In 1992, she was honored by the *St. John Business and Professional Women's Organization* as their "Woman of the Year." No one on St. John was surprised.

When asked if she had a unifying philosophy of life — or a special philosophy of business — she immediately responded without distinguishing between the two, "Service."

She's very active in various charitable community events.

The year she headed up the United Way fundraising efforts on St. John — it set a record. Over the years, she's organized dozens of fundraisers for St. Johnians with serious medical problems. Some of her efforts have been highly visible; many have been invisible. A few have been so subtle that even the people directly involved aren't quite sure what happened.

Recently a local government worker — a particularly hard working, efficient, friendly man — felt unappreciated by his employers. On an almost daily basis for years he'd gone beyond the strict call of duty — and yet nobody seemed to care.

Cid found out, and with a few phone calls managed to arrange to have the man rewarded for all his sterling service — at least in some small, symbolic way. "Everyone wants to feel they're appreciated, and this guy certainly is. He helps everyone on the island out almost every day. It was just a matter of getting the community together to tell him how much we appreciate his efforts."

There she goes again. Cid is — by training, degree, and temperament — the ultimate social worker. At times it appears her profit-making business is just an efficient financial instrument to raise the necessary funds to finance her many worthy causes.

In many ways, she's a classic Utopian. She's using capitalism to create enough wealth to share. Sometimes it's difficult to decide whether Cid is old fashioned, too new fangled, or just plain nuts. Sometimes, she can't seem to decide herself.

Of course, Cid's unique personality inspires a fierce devotion on the part of her employees. They don't just work *for* Cid, they work *with* her... and she with them.

The staff of Connections has, well... the public persona of the company is distinctly feminine without being girlish.

The office has a certain texture and taste — kinda like a female version of the male "buddy-films." Cid and her trusty sidekick Good Ole Mary Pat. Butch Cassidy & the Sun Dance Kid. Yeah. Like that.

These women are obviously having fun. They're actually enjoying themselves while making money. They laugh a lot; and chat. Even gossip sometimes. Yes, they're here to serve; no, they're not subservient.

Mary Pat (manager and wit extrordinaire) has been with Cid almost from the beginning. Her devotion to Cid & Company is plain. In many ways, Mary Pat is more intent on Cid making a profit than Cid is.

Although they have radically different personalities — and quite divergent lifestyles — they mesh almost perfectly on the job. Co-workers. Friends. Pals.

Family.

That's it: Connections is a business staffed by a wonderfully wacky bunch of weird sisters. Sometimes they're like the Six Saintly Sisters of Salvation & Mercy. Other times they're more like the Twisted Sisters...

The list of past and present employees include Chriss Benvie, Adele Berchem, Peg Cunningham, Linda Davies, June Devisfruto, Wendy Don, Wendy Durham, Sharon English, Nina Frankel, Donna Hardy, Paula Kemp, Tonya Martin, Caroline Morrison, Diana McCallum, Kate Norfleet, Linda Pinto, Vicky Rogers, Mary Pat Sica-Brown, Lois Smith, Julienne Schuh, Wendy Swolinski, Barbie Trailer, Jean Vance, Marilyn Windrow...

When asked about some of the people who helped her most, Cid immediately mentions her landlord, Theovald "Mooie" Moorehead. "He believed in me from the very beginning, and has been a steadfast source of assurance. He gave me my big break when he allowed me to move from my tiny upstairs office to my present location."

Most people hate their landlords; Cid sends hers "thank you" notes with the rental check.

She even says nice things about the Post Office and Phone Company, for gosh sakes.

Cid isn't one to be too hemmed in by conventional thinking. In fact, her first employee at CONNECTIONS was deaf.

This wasn't normally a problem; Cid answered the phone and her deaf employee took care of the typing and other clerical work. (This was during the first few weeks she was in business.) But one day there was an emergency, and Cid had to leave the office for a few minutes.

As soon as she left, a fellow came in off the street to sign up for answering service. The deaf women could read lips, and understood what the man was saying. He said, "I'd like to sign up for answering service." Then, noting the phones were all ringing, he said, "Why aren't you answering the phone?"

The deaf woman said, "Fine. Here's the application. It's twenty a month." Then, not knowing what else to say, she blurted, "Because I'm deaf."

"Is this a joke?" he asked.

"No," she said, "It's St. John."

Cid is hopeful about the future of the quality of life on St. John. "We *can* solve our problems, but I believe that the community of St. John should be taking a more active role in shaping its own future. I'm an activist. I believe the people of St. John have a right to determine their own future. We can stop bad things from happening, and we can start good things happening. We have the power if we but use it."

She pauses, and thinks. "If your cause is just, you can move mountains."

"However, if we have no long range plan — if it's all just slap-together development — we're in trouble. St. John will soon cease to be this special place that we all love and admire so much. You know, St. Johnians are really *proud* to be St. Johnians. I don't want us to lose that pride — I don't want everyone to forget this is Love City."

"But we have a severe drug and crime problem. Crack deals go down right outside my office window every day. If the people of St. John don't do something to stop this activity — then it will continue to increase. And the related violence that goes along with it will escalate. Does someone have to be killed before something is done?"

"We're got some great police officers on St. John, but some of them have a curious attitude. It's as if some of them want to deny that anything is ever wrong. Once I called about a noise problem at four in the morning, and held my phone outside my bedroom window so the officer could hear how loud it was. His response was, 'How do I know you're not holding the phone up to a radio speaker, lady?' That struck me as a rather strange question."

When asked how she wants to be remembered by future St. Johnians, Cid quickly replies, "As someone who loved St. John. As someone who loved this island, this community, these families."

"The best part of living on St. John is the people. Many of my friends here seem more like family. There's a lot of love. I'm where I want to be."

It's fair to say that for many of the people on St. John, Cid Hamling is a special women. Her opinion is widely respected throughout the community, and she earned that respect the old fashioned, non-trendy way — by hard work. Cid has paid her dues on every level.

All in all, not bad — especially for a young women who came to these islands vowing never to be anyone's secretary.

Andromeada Childs: Island Daughter

by Susan Barry

Andromeada Childs is the quintessential St. Johnian. She carries a sense of the island deep within her; it is in her gait, her warm smile and her gentle laughter. St. John is forever a part of Andro, and Andro and her family continue to be an important part of St. John.

As the director of the Elaine I. Sprauve Museum in Cruz Bay, Andro was able to share her love for St. John on a daily basis for my years. For many of the museum's patrons, conversing with Andro was like unexpectedly taking a stroll through another time and a slightly different place — a stroll through old St. John.

"My earliest memories? There wasn't much happening in Cruz Bay. There were just a few families. I don't think we had ten houses in the area. You didn't really see too many people. There were no cars. It was mostly bush, and there were peacocks and goats and sheep running around the road.

"The Moorehead and Keating families were right in Cruz Bay Square — where we called the Yard. Then there were the Sprauves and Boynes and some folks who have passed away since; Aunt Liz (Mary Ann Elizabeth Richards) and Mrs. Richards and Mr. and Mrs. Roach, the Rhoades, and Mrs. Harvey. There was the Battery, of course. I guess that was about it.

"It was a special treat to go to Coral Bay. Usually you only went on Easter Monday. It took so long to get there because it was so far away. It wasn't as close as it is now. Now it's like fifteen, twenty minutes. Then most people would walk or would ride a horse or donkey.

"People from Coral Bay came down early in the morning to avoid the sun. They often started out when it was still dark, what they used to call 'foreday' — before dawn. People would rise early and go to bed early. There was no electricity. We used lamps and a few candles.

"They'd probably find out a few day's before that a boat was going to St. Thomas. They'd leave Coral Bay early in the morning and come down and wait. Many times the boat didn't go, maybe there was no wind or something turned up. And so the people waiting would have to go back home.

"People on St. John used messages a lot. If you were going to St. Thomas, you would inform your neighbors and family. They'd write up a shopping list for you. I remember when I needed shoes — I've always had large feet — my mother (Myra Keating-Smith) would send to St. Thomas to buy shoes for me. Very often the shoes would be too tight. Now I've always been very vain and so even if they were a little too tight — I'd still wear them. They were new and pretty and that's all I wanted. So my mother would send the list for food, clothing, medicine — whatever we needed — that's how it was done. So there was no need for everybody to go. One person went and picked up for everybody.

"It was exciting when the boat returned. You knew you were getting some special things but you didn't know exactly what. But people knew you well enough to know whether you would like this or like that. They usually brought back the right thing.

"But you knew when the boat was coming back because sometimes they would blow a conch shell. You'd hear the conch shell and — Oh! — you'd go down by the dock and look around. 'Is the boat coming?' Sometimes that boat would be out there for the longest while — tacking — going back and forth to get in. And you'd be waiting.

"You'd go out and you'd look and you'd come back and you'd look again and then sometimes you'd have to go to bed. When you heard voices — and you knew the menfolk were home — you'd get back up. You'd be so excited to see what they'd bring.

"I remember my Uncle (Eddie Moorehead) would always bring back Chicklets for me. There were two in a pack. They were such a treat.

"When it was somebody's birthday we'd get up early in the morning and pick flowers. My mother and aunt (Andromeada Keating-Titley) would make a bouquet and put it in a vase with a doily on a tray.

"You would take it over to the person's house and sing 'Happy Birthday' to them and give them a hug and a kiss. You'd say, 'Mom and Aunt Meade will see you in the afternoon and they send Happy Birthday from everybody.' Later in the day you went back for a little social — a tart and cake and a little lemonade or something to drink. During the day other people would have sent bouquets and you'd see them on the piano and on the table in the little parlor. It was nice. I remember that as a very special thing.

"Then later on in the week they'd send back the vase and doily and the tray because these had to make the rounds for everybody. It was a good custom.

"You looked out for everybody else. There was concern for each other. If you didn't see someone you would send the children over to say, 'Are you okay?' and 'Momma said, How are you doing' or 'Do you need me to do an errand?' or 'Is there anything around the house that you would like me to do for you?'

"For instance, many of the older people put their things out in the sun on a sunny day — and they'd say, 'Come help me on Saturday to put some things out,' and you were glad to do that. You were doing something good for an older family member or an older friend, sort of lightening their chore.

"My Aunt Liz was a very dear, very special person to me. She lived right on the corner across from the (Chase) Bank. And there was Aunt Sophie and friend Olympia and my grandfather (Edward Moorehead, Sr.). But everybody was 'Cousin this' or 'Friend'. Mostly you didn't call them Mrs. Jones — you said Friend, Aunt or Cousin Sue. The relationship was a bit warmer.

"Sometimes when they were sitting with another old person they would tell stories — like, 'You remember cousin so and so and she used to do this and she used to do that?' And sometimes on moonlight nights you would sit outside on the step and somebody would come and tell stories — just passing by — they would come in and sit down and tell stories.

"Or maybe the family would be sitting around and they would start, 'Oh, you remember such and such a thing?' There was always an older relative who was quite a show person — who did dramatic things and would exaggerate. The storyteller wouldn't just tell the story, they'd act it out. It was always about people you knew, a good family friend or relative, or something like that.

"They were always funny stories. I remember my Uncle Eddie used to tell stories about these two older relatives in St. Thomas at Water Bay. They'd have you screaming. You'd be laughing so hard that you'd be crying. Then somebody else would hear you laughing — because remember this was a quiet little area you're talking about — and they'd come over to see what was happening and they'd get in on it too. Younger people enjoyed that. It was a theater in itself.

"My Mother was a nurse-midwife. I didn't go with her often unless she needed me to get something for her. She was a very professional and caring person and she did not mix the privacy of the family. Never.

"If somebody was sick they'd sometimes come down here to the little clinic we had in Cruz Bay. It was right near where the old customs house used to be. I guess ladies would come down for what they called 'lying in' when they were having a baby. I would go over in the evening to sit with them — maybe take some tea. Aunt Meade would sometimes send some tea and bread or some piece of cake. And you'd go and sit with them for an hour. One lady, I remember, would teach me prayers. We'd sing little sankeys and so forth.

"Momma traveled a lot. Sometimes we would go to bed and

when I woke up the next morning she was gone. I guess somebody was sick or having a baby or something. And sometimes it lasted awhile. There was no telling when she would come back. Sometimes I worried about her. I remember worrying about her — because I was afraid of the dark.

"Moonlight nights were always beautiful here. You can imagine how beautiful it was without electricity. But when it's dark — it's really dark. So the fact that I was afraid of the dark made it so I used to worry about my mother when she would go out and it was a dark night.

"But my mother was never afraid. In those days they talked a lot about jumbies. It frightened me. But she was never scared.

"I never saw any jumbies. But in our yard we had lots of trees, and you know how coconut trees cast some fearful shadows — really scary shadows. If a branch moved, you ran! I was always in the house as soon as it was dark. I'd make sure all my chores were done before dusk. There were so many trees that cast shadows and if you looked at a shadow hard enough you would be sure to see something.

"Now childhood has changed. Children are very outspoken these days. Sometimes I don't know whether I admire them for it or would like to break their little heads or something. They're so outspoken, so opinionated. They tell you what they think, when they think it and do whatever they want. And the things they say! You wouldn't dream of it.

"Yesterday afternoon I heard some girls talking on the dock at Red Hook. They were talking about a friend and going into details about what happened. You would never do something like that in the old days. You would keep your opinion to yourself. Or you would hush-hush to your best friend when you were gossiping. Certainly kids gossiped in my day but there was a time and place for that. You only did it with your friends and you didn't do it within hearing of any adult.

"The local calypso songs back then were called 'quailbey'. They'd stick in your mind. The children might know the words to the songs but you didn't dare sing them in front of an adult. When I was growing up singing was common. If somebody was washing their clothes in their yard, they'd sing.

"Mostly they'd sing sacred songs. Many St. Johnians had beautiful voices. You'd hear them singing from a distance and then you'd join in. But you'd never hear a child singing a calypso. It was considered rude.

"Sucking your teeth was also considered rude. You know when you kiss your teeth? You didn't do that. It meant something bad. And you didn't answer back. You wouldn't dream of it. As a matter of fact you didn't even cut your eye at an adult. You kept your head down. If you looked at an adult directly in the eye they might say you were staring at them and being rude. You knew your place. If someone told you something and you didn't like it then you just walked away and when you got out of hearing range you would say what you had to say.

"Even if the person speaking to you was not a relative that person could still grab you and march you right down to your folks and complain. Then you got it twice.

"But as a child you got to hear everything. My Aunt Liz and her friend — they were both old ladies — they knew everything that was happening — they knew EVERYTHING!

"They would have their little gossip every afternoon. I would be right there making believe I was reading or sewing. You know, you always had a little sewing to do — and you heard everything. But you didn't dare voice your opinion or say, 'It didn't go like that.' But these kids today — children now? Oh, they tell you, they correct you and tell you, 'No, it didn't go like that.'

"Back then if a child was a little presumptuous, the adults would say, 'March outside — you go outside.' They had a little expression they'd say 'Mounse your sex'. It meant 'among your own peers'. You do this in your peer group, not with us. Know your place, in other words. This is not your conversation.

"They'd chase you out in a hurry! But as long as you'd be quiet, you'd be okay. You had to be tactful about it.

"You didn't just pass it on. You'd only say it to your very best friend. 'Guess what I heard?' But if an adult asked you, 'Did you hear?' you'd say, 'No, I didn't. I don't know. I didn't hear that.' Very good politics.

"My very best friend was Inez Samuel. She and I were in the same Sunday school class. We're still good friends. There was another young lady, Greta Blyden — she lives in The States — and Harriet — we were a little clique. We still check on each other and stay in touch.

"We went to Bethany School. We walked but you didn't think about it. You had nothing else to judge by. There were no cars. There was a car, but that came along much later — a truck, in fact. I think the adults were afraid of the truck because they told us not to ride in it. But it was such a novelty that kids would take a ride anyway. Mr. Victor Sewer drove the truck. He was nice. He would stop and give you a ride.

"Now if you were coming home (from school) he'd put you out by the Seventh Day Adventist Church or before the police station. You couldn't come all the way down to your gate or anything and still make believe you walked. Nobody noticed that you came home early, I guess. It was too funny. All the kids were curious about this car and they wanted to ride in it.

"There were lots of us who went to school at Bethany. Sometimes if my Uncle Eddie was working anywhere in the area I'd get a ride with him on his horse. Some people rode a donkey, I guess, but it wasn't a regular thing. Everybody just walked.

"I remember when mangoes were in season. The boys sometimes would pick mangoes down in the ghuts. Naturally you had to be their friend or else you weren't going to get any. Then they'd share them out. They'd tease, but the were really nice.

"After school everybody had to work. It's just what you had to do. I helped out my Aunt Meade at home. When you came home from school they'd give you something to eat. Afterwards there were dishes that had to be washed or you'd have to sweep or something.

"The yard always had to be kept well swept. Every house had a special yard broom. There was no trash around because people were basically caring and interested in the community.

"Whatever brown paper was around was recycled. Whenever people would go from one place to another they would take a little package of spice or something. Yeah, it was sharing, which was really nice. I remember that very specially. People would send little packages — a little package of something insignificant — but in those days it meant a lot. They would send salt from the Salt

Pond, or maybe a few bananas or fruit — that sort of thing.

"When they would bring it you'd send something back with them — whatever you put together — or whatever you could find. Today it wouldn't have any significance to you and to me. But in those days it meant a lot. It was sharing, it was caring. It was a way of touching. I'm thinking about you. I love you.

"We had a guest house, and after school I'd often have to go over to dust it. 'Go dust the beds,' they'd say. You know those four-poster beds? They had to shine. 'Go dust the parlour.' You had to dust several times a week because dust was forever.

"My mother believed in those little dust brooms. You had to get down on your knees to use them. You had to get down under those four-poster beds to get in every corner. You swept and you dusted. Gracious. I didn't like the dusting part too much. I'd hide under the bed a lot.

"You know where Stitches and the restaurant (JJ's Texas Barbecue) is? That was our guest house. My mother's house was where Connections is.

"People came to stay at the guest house during the summer months. We had regular guests who would come in July. They were mostly from Massachusetts of the Eastern sea coast. We didn't have many other tourists — nothing like you have now. In those days not many folks traveled. People didn't have that kind of money.

"We had an older white couple that lived at my Uncle Mooie's house, Their name was Rhoades. They came and they stayed. I don't remember if they had planned to stay or just got here and couldn't go back.

"When she got sick and died, we took care of him. My Aunt Meade prepared his meals. We'd go over to see if he was okay. In the morning she would send over one of the children to check on Mr. Rhoades. We called him 'Old Rhoades.''How is Old Rhoades?' We didn't call him that to his face — you know children. He prepared his own breakfast, which was light. But Aunt Meade would send his lunch and his supper and then see that he was okay. He was old and feeble but he was also nice. I think he was a writer.

"And then there was Miss Helen, Helen Payne. I knew Miss

Helen as long as I knew myself. And Mr. Peter — which was Peter Dohm, you know, the old man that died? I remembered him a lot.

"When folks would come to visit they would talk about different things. Now, when I say people from Massachusetts, I'm not talking about a lot of people. I'm talking about two or three. I have to make that clear. The guest house wasn't always filled up. But when they came down here they would tell you stories. Mostly they were writers and artists. A lot of times they would sit on the beach and draw or up in the hills and stay for most of the day and then they would come back and show you the things that they had drawn. It was interesting.

"They'd tell you about life in The States. You'd say, 'Oh, tell me about this...' and they would. I was always very inquisitive. I remember once I asked a young man if he prayed — but I asked at the wrong time because this lady Mary that worked for my Aunt Meade overheard me. She went and complained and I got a good slap for that.

"I was named after my mother's twin sister. Aunt Meade took care of us. Momma worked and Aunt Meade stayed home. She took care of us. Aunt Meade took care of the business too. Aunt Meade said do something — you did it. Aunt Meade had the final say.

"It wasn't 'That's my mother and you're not my mother.' That never happened. As a matter of fact I don't even remember that coming up in my mind. If I had done something wrong Aunt Meade would grab me and give me a beating in a hurry. My uncles and my grandfather told me what to do too, and I did it.

"Our living house was where Connections is now. That whole area from Connections to the Backyard was where we lived. We had a living room, a sitting room and four bedrooms. Then we had a kitchen, dining room and pantry down where the restaurant used to be (which is now Meada's Shopping Plaza). We didn't eat in our living house. No food was ever brought there unless someone was sick. Then we'd bring a tray.

"We had a dining room. There was an adult table and we had a children's table too. There was myself and two of my cousins from New York and another little girl that lived with us who was my

Aunt's godchild.

"As we got older we could sit at the grown up table. We had to set the table every day. We'd set it for breakfast with a mat and napkin — you had to set a regular table. And people ate breakfast at different times. My grandfather and uncles ate early. As they ate you removed their dishes and then the table was cleared until the next meal and then it had to be set again.

"After dinner everything was cleaned up. All the rooms were cleared and all the dishes put away. The fire hearts (hearths) were cleaned out too. We had three of them. You had to clean out the cinders and then you locked up.

"One of my favorite memories is of my Aunt Meada baking. She would get up at three or four o'clock in the morning and go down in the kitchen. I'd take my cover and pillow and go with her. I'd keep her company. The bread had to set and you had to let it raise and then you had to put it down — and then do it all again. It was a long process. Sometimes she'd give me a little piece of dough. I'd liked that. During the holidays we would be cooking and baking and doing things like forever. The day was more than twenty-four hours long.

"I like to eat. When I was a child I had a good appetite. I would work with Aunt Meade in the kitchen when she cooked and she used lots of pots and pans. I would clean up behind her. I'd help her peel things, and so forth.

"If we had guests we had to set the dining table on the guest house porch. That is where the guests ate. You had to take the food over on a tray.

"When we were completely finished cleaning up, then Aunt Meade and I would eat. She didn't like you eating while you were working. You weren't allowed to do that. You could eat either before or after.

"There was always a lot of work to do — especially at holiday time. There was the silver to clean and the good dishes to take down. Afterwards, these dishes had to be repacked carefully, and put back in the box exactly the way they had been — between little pieces of cardboard.

"During the holidays people would stop by from other parts of the island. They came to serenade. These days mostly young people and children serenade, but then it was adults. You were expecting them so you were prepared. They'd sing and then come in and you'd feed them — serve them whatever, then they'd stay a little while and then they'd go on to somebody else.

"Weddings were a big thing — and it was always so hot. I remember being in a wedding. There were two things I remember about weddings. It was always hot and my feet always hurt. My shoes were never comfortable — I mean, they were pretty shoes — but they always hurt my feet. You stand on one foot for awhile and ease them out and then stand on the other foot awhile. And it was so hot and you were wearing all this satin slip and satin bodice and a frilly dress. You were dressed to the hilt but, gosh, it was hot.

"And there was so much to eat! There was always goat and pig and mutton and beef. There was never-ending food. And cakes, oh my gosh, the sweets were never-ending. All kinds of cakes and all kinds of tarts. In those days I think the cakes were heavier than they are now and the icing was hard with all those silver and spangles. I used to love that. And the icing was so hard. I think the icing preserved the cake. Icing these days is fluffy and soft but you could have killed someone with that icing in the old days.

"Can you imagine a wedding at Bethany Church? You were either Lutheran or Moravian. There were a few people that were Seventh Day Adventists but mostly everybody was Lutheran or Moravian in those days — with the exception of my grandfather — who was the only Catholic on St. John.

"But suppose the wedding was up at Bethany. You would walk all the way up to Bethany Church in that heat in those clothes. Then they would have the ceremony, which was long and drawn out, and then they'd march back down if the reception was in Cruz Bay.

"How did you know what was happening on the outside world? You read a lot. I remember a newspaper we got at school called 'Current Events' and that kept you pretty much up on what was happening in The States. Plus, you got magazines.

"People didn't go back and forth to The States then as much as they do now. Those people who went to The States would live there for years before they made their first trip back. It wasn't like now, where you can just go up for a weekend. It was very expensive and it took a long time. It was like seven or eight hours traveling. You had to stop in Puerto Rico and you had to stop in Cuba and then in Florida. I was a never-ending trip.

"I remember when I left in 1946 when I went to New York. I left before day. We went to Puerto Rico the day before and we stayed overnight. I didn't get to New York until 'foreday' the next day. It was like 4 o'clock the next morning. It was an all-day trip.

"I went by plane and we stopped in Cuba and Miami. In those days a plane would develop some kind of trouble and it would have to stay awhile and get repaired. I imagine I was supposed to arrive in New York at 6 or 7 o'clock at night.

"When I went to The States I expected a magnificent place. It was always just The States whether you were talking about Florida or New York. I'd read about it, and listened to so many stories. You always wanted to meet people from The States because you knew they would dress and look different. They fascinated me.

"If somebody left and came back, then they acted like someone who had gone away. I think sometimes they just put on a performance. But you wanted to see them anyway. They always had tall tales to tell. And their experiences were always so magnificent — stories about going on a train trip to someone who wasn't even supposed to take a ride in Victor Sewer's truck were pretty thrilling.

"They're telling you how you go down these steps and you get in this thing — in these cars. And you drive forever and ever underground and you don't come out and you could even go in the stores and you don't have to come out on the street.

"I remember being told these stories and thinking, 'What? You don't have to go up on the street?' No, you don't have to go up on the street at all. You just go from one store to the other because there were some stores that were connected by a tunnel and then when you were ready you go back down and you get in your train and you go home. It all fascinated me.

"I didn't know much about fancy stores and things like that. But I knew enough to know that I couldn't wait to get in those stores. My uncle took me to the Woolworth's store, and, oh God, that was heaven. I remember being fascinated by those little barrettes, you know, that little kids put in their hair. I had never seen this big a

Woolworth store. This was a big treat and I would never forget that experience. I guess he spent about ten dollars on me. I thought that was a lot of money. Besides, the store was so pretty and it smelled good. It was a whole new experience for me.

"Snow. I woke up and there was snow coming down. I had been told that it looked like the inside of a feather pillow. It was a nice, bright, sunny day and this snow was coming down and I just ran out in my slippers and it was so cold — it was such a difference.

"I remember how my mother prepared me for the winter. You know those plaid blankets? She had asked somebody to make me a robe out of one of those blankets. This seamstress, this lady that sewed for my mother, Miss Ella, made me a robe. It lasted a long time. She was a very good seamstress. It was warm. I don't remember feeling the cold so much back then but as I got older I felt it more.

"Yes, you miss home. But you meet people. When you went to New York the people from the islands had their way of getting together. The Transfiguration Lutheran Church in New York was the meeting place. You'd see a lot of familiar faces.

"In my case I hadn't known this one aunt before I arrived. My mother had spoken about her a lot and sort of prepared me. I had known the cousins because they had lived here for a while. But people were warm. They carried that warmth with them even to The States. They made you feel welcome.

"It was a funny thing. You were lonesome but there was a special camaraderie among people from the islands. They sort of came together. A friend of my mother's visited me when I first arrived. This was in December. It was the middle of winter and I was cold. This friend of my mother's had gone through her closet and picked out some warm things for me. I remember this especially because it was such a very very kind thing. She brought me warm underwear and other clothing.

"It was a way of looking out for one another. There's a special feeling that you get from those kinds of things. I still remember that special feeling. Somebody cared.

"I was in New York about 30 years. I came back home to St. John for the first time 20 years later. People didn't go back and forth as much then. When people came to visit they stayed for a few months because they weren't coming right back. It was expensive. It was like $800 for a one-way ticket. That was a lot of money. People didn't have that kind of money in those days. It took you several years to save. So there was no going back and forth really.

"When I came back for the first time, oh my God, there were houses in places where I had never even thought people would build. It was hard to imagine.

"And — there was electricity. Lights went on at 6 p.m. and off at 9 p.m. There was a little basketball court by our Cruz Bay Park where the young men used to play. We would gather there and talk. "Some of my friends had gotten married and had children. People came to visit me. They were really nice. They'd hear you were home and so they came to see you and they probably bought you a little gift or some fruit.

"I was so happy to get home even though everybody looked different and the place looked different. There was a movie theater and a dance hall. There had been no dance halls when I left. So there was someplace to go. Miss Huldah Sewer had a dance hall where the Tamarind Court is today and the Hilltop was a dance hall. So it was nice. It was happening.

"Maybe I should back up and not say a movie theater. It sounds like the real thing. But you could see a movie on a Thursday night. That was something.

"I saw my first movie in New York. I was excited. It was 'Sinbad the Sailor'. I was so happy to see it I sat through it twice. In those days they didn't empty the theater. I was fascinated. I really enjoyed it. My folks were having a fit because we went to the movies on a Saturday afternoon matinee and you were expected home at a certain time. I was with my two cousins. But I was so excited. 'Please, please,' I begged them to stay.

"When we got home we were in a lot of trouble and the punishment was we couldn't go back for a long time. But I think that my aunt probably didn't understand that this was my first time in a movie house and I just wanted to see it again. Young people are fascinated, used to be, by the movies. Actors and actresses were the epitome of excitement and grandeur and so forth.

"I came back to St. John for the first time in 1966. I missed

New York, but I loved St. John. I loved meeting the folks I hadn't seen in so long. It was just this great feeling. I wanted then to come back home some day to stay. So I went back and told my husband, 'One of these days we must retire to St. John.' I filled him up so. I was so in love with it and told him all about it and he got excited too. He wanted to see it. So he made a trip and he fell madly in love with the place too and he decided that, 'Yes, we would come back.' So we came back home sooner than I had thought we would be able to. It was a good feeling.

"But adjusting when you come back — when it's for real— was kind of hard because I was leaving friends and family up there. And I missed some of the conveniences of New York, like being able to run downtown and pick something up. It was different. It took me a while to adjust.

"And yes, yes the people here were very caring — even then. This still goes on among certain some people here. There are still people who share and care about each other. Here. Now.

"I see that when my mother is here mainly. When Momma is here somebody is always sending her a little package with a little something in it. Now, the funny thing is that my mother was not the cook. I don't think I've ever eaten a meal that my mother cooked as a child. Never. My Aunt Meade took care of that. And then when my Aunt Meade died my Momma had to begin to do little things in the kitchen like making soup.

"I remember a friend of hers would make her little packages of seasonings — a little bit of this and a little bit of that. A little something like some pigeon peas from the garden. Well, then Momma would make up a little package of something to share in return. So it's still going on. Not on as wide a scale as it used to before, but it still happens.

"People have gotten modernized, Americanized, so they're only interested in themselves. They don't have the time to care anymore.

"Every morning my mother will call certain people. 'How are you today?' They do the same with her. But some people don't carry on that tradition of touching base with each other like old days — and yet we have telephones now. So there's no excuse, really. Because in those days you didn't have a phone. You'd have to run around and visit. But even with the telephones we don't have the time to care and share.

"We have cars. We have taxis. We have telephones. But we don't seem to have time to visit anymore. As a matter of fact people are so busy these days they don't even have time to stand and talk with somebody. You see them in the bank or the post office or on the way to the ferry and maybe you make a little fast conversation. 'We must get together' That's about it. You don't expect this on St. John.

"But look at all the shops we now have in Cruz Bay. In my day, we didn't even have a shoe store. We didn't have a clothing store. We didn't have a candy store...

"...There was a lady that made homemade candy who lived down by Miss Elaine's (Miss Elaine I. Sprauve) house. When she made candy — once a week — that was a treat. If somebody gave you five cents or twenty-five cents that was a big thing back then. Today, you can't give a little child fifty cents. What are they going to buy? So St. John is almost like a metropolis now. You have bars, you have grocery stores, supermarkets, hat stores, boutiques. We have come a long way.

"If I could bring something forward from My St. John? It would begin with family relations and friends — the extended family. That feeling of caring and sharing. It isn't what you had or what you gave to somebody, but it was that you were touching and extending yourself to them and they to you. I think that if you have that you have all the rest.

"We have everything else we need — all the material things. But we don't have that one thing that we could really use more of. That feeling of caring.

"When I first came back home they used to have fish frys. Those were so nice. They were like family gatherings. People would bring their children. I don't know if people went there to eat or not, but it was a good feeling. There was music and you would dance and you'd have a few drinks and have a good time — everybody — the whole community, white, black, everybody was one and you had this nice feeling. A feeling that everybody was one and everybody was getting along and pulling on the same team.

"But now, things have changed so that you don't know the other fellow. You don't care. You don't feel that you want to be bothered stretching out your hand or saying hello.

"It could be because so many people are just coming and going. I usually say hello to people when I see them. I don't care if I know them or not. If I'm passing by I'll say, 'Good morning' or 'Good afternoon, how are you?' Some people will answer and some won't and I don't feel badly if they don't because they're not accustomed to it. They're accustomed to rushing by and minding their own affairs and maybe if you say hello, they might think you want something. But you know that you're just saying, 'Hi!' I like to do that. A little community like this — which is just one square block — we could have a little more friendship than we do.

"It is a fact that you don't really know a lot of the people today because they're so much in transit. They don't stay very long. Even the businesses don't. So you can't really expect people to make any kind of lasting relationships. Why bother? So, in a sense, I understand. They think, I'm only here for a few months, so why extend yourself? Mind your business, do your own thing and move on.

"But I guess that attitude rubs off on all of us.

"The way we used to maintain that community feeling here on St. John was by having fish frys and other community get-togethers. Everyone came together at church and school affairs. Now people are so busy establishing a little business or setting up their family that they don't have the time for such things. They probably would like to, at least in some instances. But they don't extend themselves.

"There's so much I wish for the young people of St. John. I wish that our young people would be a little bit more mannerly. There's a softness that's gone. The edges are too rough, coarse. Loud. Cursing. No self-respect. They need exposure to some of the social graces. 'Thank you'. A nice smile. Not so arrogant and so mean — coming across mean when, basically, they're not. We have some nice young people. Their heart is in the right place but they don't express themselves in a soft, graceful manner.

"It probably comes from lack of self-confidence or 'attitude'. It makes you a 'cat' as they say or it makes you big in the sight of others. But I think that when they act that way they're only big in the sight of their peers and not by anyone else. However, if they tried a little good manners, they would be more accepted by other people, instead of just in their own little circle. So I would wish for them gentleness.

"I would also wish for them that they would set high goals for themselves. Something to achieve.

"I guess the fact that parents are not at home as much anymore is having an effect. People have to work two and three jobs so they don't have much time to spend with their children. The children have to raise themselves.

"I wish today's kids didn't watch so many TV shows and movies. The actors and singers are becoming their role models. They shouldn't be. Their role models should be at home. People shouldn't look to someone they don't know. I don't care if they're the same color. Your role models should be the people who are touching you on a regular basis. It's the people right here around you. That's who you are and that's where they are.

Ivan and I
by
Doris Jadan

Many current St. John residents were born elsewhere. I was born on June 18, 1925, in Tuscaloosa, Alabama. Thirty years later, on June 18, 1955, my Russian husband Ivan and I finally "reached" St. John. We've been living here ever since. A number of interesting things happened along the way. I'll just mention a few of the highlights.

While I "escaped" from Alabama at age seven in 1932, my husband Ivan didn't manage to escape from the Soviet Union until 1941. He was 39 years old at the time. Music is what brought us together.

I've always been interested in music, especially Russian music and ballet. I was only five years old when I first saw the legendary Anna Pavlova dance in Birmingham, Alabama. Afterwards, I did my best to imitate her movements. But I didn't have any ballet shoes, so I just rose straight up on my bare toes and danced, sort of.

Hearing great music throughout my childhood may have presaged my life as the wife of Ivan Jadan, the great Russian tenor of this century. I remember as a child the excitement of listening to the Saturday afternoon radio broadcasts of the Metropolitan Opera sponsored by Texaco. My mother and I went to the home of a lovely, silver-haired friend in Dallas, Mrs. Witherspoon. I heard on the radio the debut of Kirsten Flagstad, the incomparable Wagnerian soprano. Later when we were living in Washington, D.C., I saw and heard Flagstad with Lauritz Melchior in Wagner's Tristan and Isolde. I was by then ten years of age. We were seated in the front row and I counted every hair on the great Heldentenor's chest.

Loving music as I did, you may wonder if I ever learned to play an instrument. Alas, I did not. In my family, each of my three older sisters was given music instruction — all to no avail. By the time I came along, it was decided that the best musical career for me was to be a good listener.

I attended Lakeview Elementary School in Birmingham. Like most of the rest of Alabama, this school had no lake to view. After Lakeview, I accompanied my mother on a year long cruise. Then I attended the John Quincy Adams School in D.C. We next moved to New Orleans, and I smelled the magnolias outside the windows of my algebra class at the Louise Schaumburg McGehee School for Girls on Prytania Street. I won a scholarship to Vassar in 1943-45, where I majored in medieval history. Why medieval? So I wouldn't have to nudge my way through hordes of modern history majors deep in the bowels of the library. After getting pneumonia twice at Vassar, I went to Tulane University in New Orleans where I majored in philosophy under Dr. Otis Lee, who, like me, had nearly succumbed to the desolate wet cold of Poughkeepsie. I graduated from Tulane in 1946 and was off to post war Vienna and Salzburg, Austria where my family was involved in military intelligence.

I've already told how enthralled I was with the voice of Lauritz Melchior. I heard almost all the great voices of the 1930s. I often attended operas and concerts with such singers as Raoul Jobin, Jussi Bjoerling, Tito Schipa, and Beniamino Gigli.

In 1947, near the Bavarian town of Weilheim, Germany, I first heard Ivan Jadan sing. Jadan lived at the time in a home belonging to the Barsky family, prominent Russian emigres from the 1920s. The Barsky home was a hideout for Jadan from the active efforts by the NKVD, Soviet Secret Police, who were charged with his forcible repatriation. This permission by the U.S. for the Soviets to forcibly repatriate over a million Russian refugees in Europe after World War II was one of the ugly terms of the Yalta Agreement where an ailing FDR gave his consent to this hideous violation of human rights. Our Intelligence was aware in 1947 that Ivan Jadan was number one on the list of Russians who Stalin wanted to force back to the USSR. This is why the Barkskys were hiding him.

When I first heard Ivan Jadan sing the Song of India from Rimsky-Korsakov's opera Sadko, I didn't even know his name, let alone his background as Premier Lyric Tenor of the Bolshoi Opera. But I did know immediately and unmistakably that I was listening to the most astonishing tenor voice that I had ever heard, and I had heard the best. This tenor could breathe with magic and he could shade and color every note, word, and phrase from pianisssimo to mezzo voce to fortissimo. I knew no Russian words in 1947, but even though I couldn't translate what he sang, I understood, body and soul, what he was singing about. I felt then as my father felt later when he heard Ivan Jadan sing, "No one could hear this man sing with dry eyes."

In Russia, Ivan Jadan had been officially declared an "Enemy of the Soviet Union." He was also blacklisted at Moscow's famous Bolshoi Theatre where his singing had once attracted large crowds. Even the sale and playing of his phonograph records were banned for his refusal to accept Communist doctrine. (How happy we were recently to hear many of these records collected by Ivan's son Vladik from contacts in Poland, Germany, and Russia from ardent Jadan fans.)

Concerts for Ivan were even more important than performances at the Bolshoi. His accompanist and coach was Matvei Sacharoff, uncle of Andre Sacharoff. Ivan's concert repertory was unrivaled.

Labeled "politically unreliable," Jadan was kept under strict surveillance by the Soviets. He never joined the Party. When Germany attacked Russia during World War II, Jadan decided to use the opportunity to escape from the Soviets.

He was captured by the Germans, and spent the next four years at a Versorgungshein in Germany. This was a "heim" or home for the elderly and disabled. The Germans allowed Catholic nuns to operate the facility. Fortunately for Ivan it was *not* a slave labor camp. Ivan worked raising vegetables, primarily spinach, which he never ate again until he tasted St. John kallaloo. Ivan endeared himself to the nuns by repairing bomb-blasted windows and anything else out of order, including a grandfather clock and the head nun's dislocated knee! The nuns nicknamed Ivan "the man who can do everything."

Liberated by American troops in May 1945, Jadan sang one concert for the troops arranged by the Red Cross. At first he was troubled by the soldiers' loud whistling and stamping on the floor. In Russia, such response signaled disapproval. But the GI's loved Ivan. However, since the Soviets were trying to locate and capture Ivan, it was too dangerous for him to continue to give concerts.

At one of his first American concerts in 1950 at Town Hall, *Time* magazine's critic wrote, "He sang with lyrical warmth and an expressiveness that reminded some of Caruso, and he reduced many in his audience to bravos and tears."

It was my father, Col. Sam Clabaugh, who helped make it possible for Ivan Jadan to emigrate to the U.S. Even with his contacts in the intelligence community and Washington, it took almost two years of effort. I flew from Germany to the U.S. with Ivan as his body guard.

Our time in New York in 1949 and 1950 was frightening. I was staying with a family friend from Tuscaloosa, Katie Lee Johnson. I worked by day, underground at the Rockefeller Center, selling Girl Scout equipment. One night as guests at a dinner served to us by two members of a group supposedly helping anti-Soviet refugees, Ivan and I were poisoned by arsenic in the red wine. I almost died.

Despite this incident, I'm happy to report that I retained my fondness for red wine!

Later, after we moved to Florida in 1951, an FBI agent who dated a close friend of ours told her how he was working in Manhattan when these acts of Soviet terror against Jadan were going on. The agent said it was a miracle that we made it alive to Florida.

After the arsenic incident in Manhattan, I thought the safest place for Ivan might be the home of my godfather, Carl Carmer. At the time he lived in the historic (now a museum) Octagon House at Irving-on-Hudson. Carl was a noted and respected author and folk historian, who, as a young man, had taught at the University of Alabama in Tuscaloosa. (I was christened Doris Carmer Clabaugh.) Carl, an outspoken proponent of racial equality in the 1920s, was driven out of Alabama by the Klu Klux Klan. I knew Carl would relate to the Soviet terror stalking Ivan.

The book Carl Carmer wrote after teaching in Alabama, *Stars Fell on Alabama*, was a bestseller.

Carl and his wife Betty loved Ivan on sight, and took him in immediately.

One weekend Carl gave me $35.00. He told Ivan and me to go along Second Avenue in Manhattan to buy a balalaika. A balalaika is like a Siberian ukelele. We did just that, and the balalaika we bought was one of two made for Jascha Heifetz, the great Russian violinist. We still have that balalaika! Ivan soon taught himself to play, and he loved to sing Russian folk songs for the writers and painters who came to visit the Carmers at the Octagon House.

During those months in New York, I helped arrange two Town Hall Concerts for Ivan, and also a concert at Carnegie Hall. The largely Russian emigre audiences wept and cheered. I remember especially what Rachmaninoff's widow told me. She said that "Ecstasy!" was one song her husband wrote that she had never heard. Why? "No other tenor," she explained, "has ever had the voice to sing this beautiful and difficult song."

However, regardless of Ivan's wonderful voice, 1949 and 1950 were the wrong times for any anti-Soviet Russian artist to make a successful debut in New York. This was the height of Soviet-American friendship. When the newspapers even refused to review Jadan's debut, one critic, Louis Biancolli, of the defunct World Telegram told me, "In my opinion, and I think the American people will agree with me, anyone who leaves the Soviet Union is a renegade and a deserter."

Ivan had no need to prove himself in that kind of environment. Ivan had ben risking his life for eight years to escape Soviet terror and to find freedom. He longed to breathe clean air, swim in clear water, and feel sunlight; New York was not the right place for Ivan. Ivan opted to leave New York and go with the Carmers to Cabbage Cay near Boca Grande, Florida.

Ivan worked hard at Cabbage Cay as caretaker. I worked in Tampa at Maas Brother's Department Store so we could save up enough money to get married in Tampa on June 30th, 1951. The glorious melody for our wedding march was the theme from the Great Bells at Kiev, from Rimsky-Korsakov's "Pictures at an Exhibition".

I taught school in Tampa for four years under a great principal, Sara Alice Holt. She too was quite fond of Ivan, and has since visited us on St. John. We love sharing St. John with visitors — many friends and nearly all of our relatives have visited us here at one time or another.

They, like Ivan, want to live on St. John, they think. But it was only an Ivan who could have announced, "I stay here!" way back in June 1955, before he even stepped off the boat bringing us here for a week's vacation with a couple from Tampa. When Ivan said, "I stay here!" I knew he meant just that. He had, after all, throughout his life made firm, unconventional decisions that turned out for the best — like escaping from the Soviet Union in December of 1941.

There are two great adventures from my childhood which made arriving in St. John in 1955 seem like coming home.

The island's natural environment reminded me both of the mountains of western North Carolina and the island of Oahu.

The hills of St. John, especially the Reef Bay trail, reminded me of the green mountain trails of Banner Elk, N.C. I spent ten happy summers from ages 6 to 16 attending summer camp there.

The sparkling waters of Cruz Bay reminded me of Honolulu Harbor.

How did I get to Honolulu? On a ship. For many marvelous months in 1933-34, I traveled as a passenger (tricycle and all) aboard the naval transport ship USS *Henderson*. This cruise was a super junket for congressmen to inspect U.S. Naval bases like Hampton Roads in Virginia, Haiti, Cuba, the Panama Canal, Hawaii, Guam, the Philippines, and China (where the Navy still operated the Yangste River Patrol).

My great uncle William Bacon Oliver was head of Naval Appropriations in the House of Representatives, and so my mother and I were allowed to travel as his dependents.

Senator Jimmy Byrnes of South Carolina and Senator Dick Russell of Georgia were also on the ship. I loved to listen to their conversations. The Filipino Chef even baked me a chocolate birthday cake every week. (No wonder I grew old before my time!)

I still remember everything I saw on that cruise. I kept a diary. It was a wonderful experience.

Of course, I missed a year of school. As a result, I had trouble with long division for a number of years. Luckily, one of my fifth grade students — son of a Tampa fireman — taught me long division in 1951.

I learned more than just long division from that student. He also taught me to make sure that I listened to the children I taught. That is what has made all my years of teaching on St. John so exciting — listening and learning from my students.

On St. John I first taught (1955-56) at the old rural Bethany School. That was before we moved to the four new classrooms of the Julius E. Sprauve School in Cruz Bay. I taught for two years at Antilles School, then came back to St. John where I taught for 20 years. I retired in 1979 on disability.

Since then, as a happy spinoff from the 1933-34 naval cruise, Ivan and I have cruised the Orinoco and the Amazon. We made a trans-Atlantic voyage and a Mediterranean cruise on the *Jason* and we've cruised to every Caribbean island except Saba. We've made 9 cruises on the *Nantucket Clipper* with one cruise on the *Yorktown Clipper* to the San Blas islands and through the Canal to Costa Rica's marine parks.

Last summer Ivan and I visited Russia. It was over 51 years since his escape. We were welcomed with love and excitement. Many Russians have never forgotten that Jadan and Chaliapin were the two great Russian voices of this century.

We were met at the Moscow airport by Ivan's son Vladik and his wife Jannetta. We stayed two weeks, and had some wonderful times as we sat around a table in their tiny apartment with a number of visitors — and listened to old recordings of Ivan. We ate watermelon and sipped fine Russian champagne.

We met dozens of Russians. They all impressed us with their strength of character. Russians are a people who not only survive, but win! And they do it with energy and love.

On a two day visit to St. Petersburg, we stayed at the Astoria Hotel. This was the same hotel where Ivan had stayed in the 1930s when giving concerts. The Astoria was built in 1912, and has since been restored to its former elegance.

We ate in the Angleterre or English room, and had a marvelous meal. For an appetizer, we enjoyed perfect *pelmaynee*, or tiny spiced meat dumplings covered with thin dough in a rich homemade bullion. Our entree was *monastirski*, or monastery sturgeon. As in France, monks in Mother Russia really know how to cook.

Everywhere we looked we saw the most incredible chandeliers. I learned from a German on the flight home from Moscow that the Russian royalty loved chandeliers so much that they bought them up by the hundreds in France — and then had them crated and shipped back to Russia.

Both Ivan and I greatly admired the chandeliers of St. Petersburg, so for his birthday here on St. John I gave him a custom-made Waterford crystal chandelier for his 90th birthday. I special ordered it through Island Galleria in Mongoose Junction. It was made in Ireland.

Ivan's eyes really sparkle when that chandelier is lit. Now we have a small touch of the magic we found in St. Petersburg right here in St. John.

As I write words in early 1993, Ivan is 90 years old. He is still quite active. He awakens each morning at six o'clock, and enthusiastically announces in Russian, "Greet the light, and close the door on darkness!"

Often, we ride our golf cart to Frank Bay. Ivan cautions me to go slow and avoid potholes. "Move gently with God," he says.

One of Ivan's favorite pastimes is gardening. Once, way back in 1939, he managed to start growing a watermelon on the top of his grand piano in Moscow. This was not an easy task — the Russian evenings are quite cold. In June, he planted the watermelon at his dacha, and it did just fine. As a child in the Ukraine, Ivan also learned the basics of blacksmithing from his grandfather and uncle.

These talents came in handy when Ivan worked at Caneel Bay. He not only grew their papayas, but also custom made many of their tools. This was in 1955, and Ivan made 55 cents an hour. His co-workers at that time thought that it was a waste of time to plant lignumvitae because it grew so slowly — but Ivan planted hundreds of trees which are blooming trees today.

Ivan has always loved the water, and enjoyed swimming. He has even acted as a marine choreographer when he taught one pet octopus Pavlova to perform a graceful underwater ballet!

Ivan still sings occasionally. He held a concert on St. John in 1966. In September of 1991, he sang two folk songs, *Yamshik* and *Choopchik*, to a small gathering of friends in Washington, D.C. on his 89th birthday. Guests included fans who had heard him sing in Riga, Latvia, back in 1937.

His most recent public singing was in 1992 on Tortola. He was visiting the famous plastic surgeon Dr. Robin Tattersall to have a small bit of skin cancer removed from his left ear tip.

Knowing something of Ivan's extraordinary career as a singer, Dr. Tattersall played a tape recording of Pavarotti during the surgery — opera for the operation, if you will.

As Pavarotti began singing the aria "Una furtiva lagrima" from Donizettis's opera, *L'Elisir d'Amore*, Ivan suddenly announced, "I know that aria!"

Dr. Tattersall was tidily stitching up Ivan's left ear tip with some 20 stitches when Ivan, lying on his side and feeling no pain, erupted in full voice.

Luckily, the acoustics in the operating room were excellent. Ivan soon overpowered poor Pavarotti. Dr. Robin Tattersall seemed to enjoy the moment. (Perhaps Pavarotti will show up for a tummy-tuck next!)

Of course, down through the years, Ivan has known a number of famous people. In 1935, the great Turkish leader Ataturk gave Ivan his personal gold monogrammed cigarette case, and declared, "You are my son — I adopt you!" (Stalin had sent Ivan and other top Russian performers to Turkey as a good will gesture.) Ivan still has Ataturk's cigarette case though he has never smoked.

Early in his career, Ivan was a protege of the famous acting coach Stanislavsky — who founded the Moscow Art Theater. Stanislavsky told the young tenor that unlike most singers, "...you have good diction!"

On St. John, Ivan became friends with nuclear physicist Robert Oppenheimer. We met Robert, Kitty, and Tony, and had some wonderful times together.

Despite Robert Oppenheimer being as gaunt as Gandhi, he enjoyed good champagne and fine food, albeit only in small sips or morsels. I remember how happy we were one evening when Ivan prepared shashlik — and Robert ate not merely a morsel but an entire skewer. Ivan had marinated and charcoal-broiled that lamb to near-perfection!

One evening, Ivan's son Alexander asked Robert what, in his opinion, were the two greatest books in the world.

Oppenheimer's answer, without a moment's hesitation was, "*The Bible*" and "*Don Quixote*." Not the *Old Testament* or the *New Testament* alone, but the *Bible* as an entity. This for Robert was the greatest book for the whole world. The dignity and simplicity of conviction with which Robert spoke at times like these were startling and always moving.

Don Quixote? Yes! Ivan understood that answer also, and has since re-read Cervantes cover to cover many times.

In spite of all the troubles that seemed to twist around Robert Oppenheimer, he kept his sense of humor. Once he and Kitty invited us to spend the day with them at Hawksnest. Ivan declined, saying he had to work on our not-yet-finished house.

An hour later, Robert showed up at our house, saying as he stood under the genip tree, "Mahomet won't come to the mountain, so the mountain has come to Mahomet!"

We only saw Robert angry one time. There had been some tension between the Oppenheimers and Bob Gibney. Gibney had sold Oppenheimer the land for his St. John home. One evening when we were having supper, Ivan sang a bit. We were drinking wine, merry but sober. Gibney came over, and rather rudely interrupted. I don't even remember what specific issue Gibney raised. I was frozen. The frail body of Robert Oppenheimer seemed suddenly ten feet tall. His splendid blue eyes shot fire as he told Gibney to leave and never return.

One evening, Robert and Kitty visited our house for dinner. Ivan showed Robert a small Hawksbill turtle from Cruz Bay with the initial 'I' carved on its shell to identify it in years to come. (This was before the days of turtle tagging.)

We didn't explain why we had the turtle or our plan to release it when we showed it to Robert.

Robert winced. He and Kitty thought we might be planning to kill the turtle. Kitty told me how Robert had righted a tortoise which had been overturned in the desert during the first atomic blast.

We quickly explained we intended to put the turtle back in the sea. In fact, we did so right then and there, before supper. Today I have only the picture of Ivan and the turtle. I wish we also had a picture of Robert and the tortoise.

Robert Oppenheimer was a great man. We remember him with love, laughter, and tears — and we share his hope for man's salvation through the grace of God.

Like Ivan always says, "Move gently with God!"

Doris Jadan can often be spotted hot-rodding her golf cart around the streets of Cruz Bay. She's written a number of books over the years. Her Natural History of St. John *is still in print.*

Publisher's Note: Robert Oppenheimer is commonly referred to as "the father of the atomic bomb." He was in charge of the brilliant group of scientists in Los Alamos, New Mexico which conceived, developed, built, and tested the first nuclear devices in the early 1940s. Later, he strongly opposed the development of the more powerful hydrogen bomb. He was a highly controversial figure; in 1953 the Atomic Energy Commission suspended him as an alleged security risk.

Evidently, he was a man who had many friends-- and some enemies. When he died in 1967, *Life* magazine reported: "Robert Oppenheimer went to his grave an equivocal man, loved and hated, admired and reviled by intelligent, public-spirited people whose opposite opinions deserve equal respect. Only a few months ago, when it was already known that he was extremely ill and probably would soon die, a distinguished mathematician could say with cold conviction, "Frankly, I hate his guts"; while a distinguished physicist could say, with tears in his eyes, "I love him."

For another perspective on Oppenheimer, see Nancy Gibney's piece entitled *Finding Out Different* which follows.

Finding Out Different
by Nancy Gibney

"Nancy, in profile and in this poor light, you rather resemble a former hostess of mine, the Queen of Greece." — J. Robert Oppenheimer

In my youth I was incorrigibly fond of asking people to stay at Hawksnest, our home on St. John in the Virgin Islands. The summer of 1959 this habit got me into some very thick soup. My husband Robert Gibney had expected as much; but Gibney always expected — indeed hoped — for the worst, and occasionally he was disappointed. Not so, that summer. Of all the explosive invitations I have ever issued, that one turned out to be the Bomb.

Two years before, we had sold a little land at the east end of our beach to the atomic physicist J. Robert Oppenheimer and his wife Kitty. They lived in Princeton where Oppenheimer was then directing the Institute for Advanced Studies; *in absentia* they were trying to build an unwieldy beach cottage designed for them by Wallace Harrison, who had previous architectural experience designing the United Nations buildings in New York.

For several years the Oppenheimers had been spending vacations on St. John, staying at Trunk Bay, a small guest house on a magnificent beach near Hawksnest on the north shore. Now Trunk Bay had been sold to the new Virgin Islands National Park and the guest house had ceased to operate. Kitty wrote to me in despair: they wanted to come down in June and check on the putative progress of their construction; where could they possibly stay? They thought of themselves as old island hands, and scorned the modern conveniences of Caneel Bay Plantation, St. John's only hotel.

Gibney and I had lived in the islands ever since we first saw them on our honeymoon in 1946, and there was nothing modern or convenient about us. At Hawksnest we had five decaying beds and three demanding children, the youngest of them a year old. We were in no position to accommodate any visitors; even I, in my *folie d'hotesse*, knew that. But it occurred to me that our two sons might vacate their room for a few days: one of them could have my bed, the other the living room sofa. I could sleep on a pad on the terrace floor; I'd forgotten how to sleep much anyway. I was not so rash as to think I could cook for the Oppenheimers. I had dined with them once in Princeton, and seen their sensitive quivering approach to cuisine. But Kitty could have "kitchen privileges" — grotesque words to use in connection with our underprivileged kitchen. At least they would be close to their construction site, and the convenience of that should compensate for many inconveniences.

In great hesitation and humility (I was much in awe of Robert; Kitty was known to be "difficult" but I thought I had tact enough for two), I wrote and offered them the use of the boys' room if it would do them any good at all.

Kitty promptly wrote back accepting my offer. Their fourteen-year-old daughter and a school chum of hers were coming with them. They understood that only one bedroom was available; the girls would bring a tent to sleep in. Alas, they probably couldn't spend the whole summer, only a month or so.

I reeled.

Gibney railed. "Oh for Christ's sake. They're going to want to *talk* all the time." Gibney dreaded solitude, but he liked the advantages of it, and insisted on silence around the house unless he himself felt moved to converse. It wasn't likely that he'd want to converse much with Oppenheimer, of whom he was emphatically not in awe. Genius I.Q.s cut no ice with Gibney. He and all his best friends and even his wife had genius I.Q.s and look at what a bunch of shitheads *we* were. To have presided over the invention of the atom bomb was no recommendation either: "For the love of God, Nancy. The man's done more mischief than anyone else in the history of the human race. And you think he's *kind? Charming?* Jesus Christ." Gibney had been much opposed to selling land to the Oppenheimers, and had yielded only because he liked our other real estate clients even less, and we were under pressure to sell something to someone: my mother had lent us the money to buy Hawksnest, and after many years of patience had hinted that she would be happy to see some of it repaid.

"They'd better buy their own fucking food," Gibney said. "We can't afford to feed four extra people."

Actually we were quite prosperous that year. Gibney had sold, for a good price, a block of stock in the family business that had paid no dividends since he inherited it in 1950; and I had written for *Good Housekeeping* and *Redbook* three of the most successful stories of my shameful pseudonymous career. These had been reprinted all over Europe, in England and South Africa and Australia, and nice little checks kept coming in. I had paid off my mother, and felt rich to be out of debt. But food is fearsomely expensive in the Virgin Islands (only vices come cheap here), and in any case I'd learned in the course of life with Gibney to be even more frugal than my New England upbringing had made me. I knew that however affluent we were at the moment, sooner or later we'd be flat broke again. So I practiced many comical economies, eating the children's left-overs, patching the patches on their pants, using Dresden plates and damask napkins on all occasions because paper plates and napkins cost money.

"Don't worry," I told Gibney. "They'll buy their own food *and* cook it."

He was just hitting his stride. "What about water, for Christ's sake? Four more people taking showers and flushing the toilets all the time? Those girls forever washing their stupid *hair*? Listen, baby, we haven't got enough water to get through the summer ourselves. And it's not going to rain again in any hurry." This was another valid complaint. We have big cisterns at Hawksnest, but the May rains had failed us that year, and for months we had been donating hundreds of gallons of water a week to the Oppenheimers' construction crew, camping out on the site.

"We'll just have to explain to them they've got to be terribly careful with water."

Gibney snorted. "Fat lot of good that ever does with guests. They'll get so nervous they'll get diarrhea and flush the toilets that much more. No fancy notions about using my Jeep either. The tires are just about shot."

"And how the hell can the ice box *handle* all that food?"

Obviously it couldn't. We had an old kerosene refrigerator, scarcely adequate for our own needs. "I've been thinking about buying an electric refrigerator," I said. At last we had public electricity on St. John, brought by underwater cable from St. Thomas. The power failed often, for long periods, but still it was an improvement on our own generator, now impotent anyway.

"I trust that you've been thinking about how you're going to get an electric refrigerator over here from St. Thomas."

We both knew very well that was men's work. "Look, Gib, I'm sorry," I said. "Of course the whole thing's impossible. *Mea culpa*. But I truly thought it would be just two people, for a few days. And cheer up — they'll hate it just as much as we do. They'll leave just as soon as they see what they're up against."

I underestimated our visitors' stamina. They saw what they were up against and then some — an exhausted, distraught and discourteous hostess into the bargain. But they stayed, vainly trying to teach me better manners and house-keeping methods, for seven hideous, hilarious weeks.

I first met the Oppenheimers in 1956, one day when I went alone up to Trunk Bay for lunch and they were on a holiday there. Robert's security clearance had been canceled two years before; I hadn't followed the case with any attention, being far more concerned at the time with infant activities than with un-American ones. I had only a dim impression that a great man had been brought low, not for his faults but for his virtues. I was curious to observe him. I saw at once that he and his wife were the most curious couple I had ever observed.

They were got up in routine tourist garb, cotton shirts and shorts and sandals, but they looked like nothing human, too thin and frail and pale for earthly life. They looked as if they were down from Mars, not Princeton; or as if some bright kid had made them with matchsticks and his ChemCraft set.

Kitty was the more humanoid of the two, although she seemed to have no features except for her dark eyes. Her voice was too deep and hoarse to emanate from her tiny chest; and helplessly weak as she was, she had the truculent stance of a heavyweight pugilist. I'd heard from other Trunk Bay guests that she had a "drinking problem" (the problem was that she drank a lot, and got drunk); and that, drunk or sober, she was often staggeringly rude. "Aren't you hot with all that hair?" she croaked at me, on introduction; then returned to her communion with a bottle of Danish beer.

Robert looked astoundingly like Pinocchio, and he moved as jerkily as a marionette on strings. But there was nothing wooden about his manner: he exuded warmth and sympathy and courtesy along with the fumes of his famous pipe. His voice was gentle, almost inaudible, and it became softer, the more he wanted to be heard. (Perhaps that bright kid had got the volume controls reversed.)

On introduction, he told me that he knew my "legend". I was enchanted to learn that I had one; like a fool, I didn't find out how it went.

He asked me what my husband did. It was not the time to explain that Gibney was a self-made failure, and that it had been hard uphill work for him, with all the talents he had, and had to fight against. I simply said that Gibney didn't actually "do" anything: but of course, living on St. John, there were many practical things that a man *had* to do. And Gibney had one real job, for a short time, bossing the maintenance at Caneel Bay. (Caneel had recently been bought by Laurance Rockefeller, and drastically expanded and revised.)

"He worked for Rockefeller?" Robert mused, with many portentous puffs at his pipe. At last, his voice a spellbinding whisper, he said, "I too have taken money for doing harm."

This struck me as a stunning one-liner, but when I later quoted it to Gibney he was not impressed. "For Christ's sake. You're in love with the little creep."

I wasn't, but I was fascinated by him. I'd never known a scientist; I'd always lived among artists, writers, editors, publishers, academic people, society people. Both Robert and Kitty (she was a fervent biologist) were types entirely new to me. I often overvalue new acquaintances, mistaking novelty for felicity; I like to imagine that I keep better company than I mostly do. Or, as a Broadway agent once confided to Gibney, "I treat every dame I meet like she was my sister until I find out different."

The Oppenheimers, their daughter "Toni" and her friend Isabelle duly arrived on a morning in June. I had labored for a solid month to be even roughly ready to receive them. I had stopped nursing my baby daughter (high time anyway; we'd been carrying on for the fun of it), finished the story I was writing in the hour a day I had to get off my feet, and concentrated all my spare time and strength on transforming the boys' room into a presentable guestroom.

I had made new lamp shades and counterpanes and mosquito nets; cleaned the lizard eggs and roach droppings out of the bureau drawers; scrubbed or painted or polished every surface; washed and ironed all the best monogrammed linen sheets and towels stashed away in the cedar chests; used reckless amounts of Clorox and Ajax on the guestroom bathroom and the shower room. I'd also cleaned and painted the kitchen and the kerosene refrigerator; and mended and washed and dyed the living room slipcovers.

This was largely wasted motion. Our house is beautiful, but it is a house-keeper's nightmare: no screens or windows or doors;

many wide-open archways that give free admittance to all the flora and fauna of tropical forest. When the weather is dry and windy, as it was that summer, I sweep the whole house and terrace eight or ten times a day, and another sweeping is indicated before I have put the broom away. Book cases and cabinets and closets would have to be cleaned at least once a week to meet the most relaxed Northern standards. I don't clean them that often.

Add to these structural hazards half a dozen cats, given to eating lizards and vomiting them up on the most elegant fabrics available; two boys, five and seven years old, tracking in dirt and sand, bleeding from cuts, spilling milk, mouthing mangoes; an ambulatory baby still in diapers; and Gibney, who never allowed anything to be thrown away. We kept not only every publication that had come into the house for thirteen years (*The London Observer, The New Statesman, Geographic, Life, Time, Vogue, Astounding Science Fiction,* and so forth) but things like empty mayonnaise jars when we already had a hundred empty mayonnaise jars; jar tops that fitted no jars we had, but that might be needed for jars of the future; mountains of junk that might come in handy someday, and did, the moment I'd sneaked it out to the dump. Gibney's German mother had been compulsively neat; no doubt in reaction, Gibney was compulsively messy.

It was impossible to get the house in order all at once, and I was deranged to try. But I tried, and by the time the Oppenheimers and their suite arrived, I had lost ten pounds and was a nervous wreck.

On arrival that June morning, they were most appreciative and courtly. I had evicted the boys from their room a couple of days before, had laid everything out in state, and sealed it off as tightly as a tomb. It was perfectly preserved when opened for our guests. This condition didn't last for five minutes. Leaves blew in, bugs flew in, cats and baby infiltrated, lint circulated. (Kitty had a sinus condition and lived in cringing horror of lint.) Robert, who had whispered "Palatial!" when the room was first revealed, began to puff rather irritably at his pipe.

I explained the acute water shortage, and the necessity for extreme care. "My God, we know about water," Kitty croaked. "You talk as if we'd never been on St. John before. Back in a second." She went into the bathroom and flushed the toilet.

I announced that I could give them tunafish sandwiches for lunch, but that thereafter they would have to provide and prepare their own food: I had my hands full with my own family. They agreed with enthusiasm. "Gib's going down to Cruz Bay this afternoon," I told them. "You can go along and pick up something for your dinner."

This brought on prodigies of pipe-puffing. "But clearly Kitty is rather tired after our journey," Robert said, his voice as soft as fur. "We shall rest and swim this afternoon. We'll simply have whatever you're having for dinner."

"But we're having spaghetti," I wailed. "And damn little of that."

He was charming about it. "We are not gluttons. And properly prepared, spaghetti is a delicacy."

"This won't be properly prepared," I assured him.

He eyed me keenly, and smiled, doubtfully, and went off to the bathroom, where he flushed the toilet.

Kitty pounced on Gibney, who had been so unwise as to come down from our little gatehouse where he spent his days in peace and quiet and unspeakable squalor. "Now you go help the girls get that tent set up," she ordered. Gibney hadn't been given an order since he left the Army. He was so astonished that he obeyed.

The girls were both fourteen years old, but seemed to have little else in common. The Oppenheimers' Toni was a dead-serious child, with beautiful smooth features, tragic dark eyes, long lustrous dark hair, and the condescending politeness of a princess. Her friend Isabelle was French, daughter of a Princeton professor — a hefty, Flemish-looking blue-eyed blonde, fully mature and quite cheerful.

"You know where those bums insisted on setting up their goddam tent?" Gibney raged when he returned from his good deed. "Behind the almond tree at the west end of the beach. For Christ's sake, where do they think we're going to swim?

Ever since the Oppenheimers' construction gang had installed itself at the east end of our beach, Gibney and I had been swimming at the west end, getting as far as possible (850 feet) away from them. After all our years of swimming in privacy, we felt it was indecent to swim, however decently covered, where we could be observed. Even now, after thirty years, the feeling persists with me. Swimming, like love-making, is a private affair. When boats anchor off the beach, I don't swim until they depart. If they don't depart and I'm dying to swim, I force myself into the water but I feel besmirched. When friends come to swim and ask if I'm going to join them, I always make excuses; once, that I had no bathing suit fit to be seen in; now, that I'm not fit to be seen in a bathing suit; half the year, that the water's too cold for me; half the year, that the sun's too hot for me. The truth is that I find group swimming as crummy as group sex.

I was appalled to think that I'd have to swim under the gaze of those girls or foreswear swimming entirely. "Well. They can't be in their tent *all* the time," I told Gibney.

I was right. They were in their tent only when we wanted to swim. The rest of the time, they were taking showers, flushing the toilet, and washing their stupid hair.

A day-by-day, play-by-play account of that preposterous summer would make a book, and a very boring one. There is nothing more tiresome than a grievance; and within a few hours of the Oppenheimers' arrival, everyone on the scene except maybe the baby had grievances to burn.

Kitty was outspoken about hers. German by birth and nature, convinced of her own superb domestic skills, lacking any imagination for the problems I faced, she was candidly disgusted by my slapdash methods and miserable results. "I used to have a cleaning woman who worked the way you do," she told me the second day of their sojourn. "I got rid of *her* in a hurry."

The girls were aggrieved because I didn't treat them with the tenderness to which they were accustomed. I gave them hundreds of oatmeal cookies I'd made for my own children, and many of their meals (they were pathetically hungry; the Oppenheimers never did get their transportation and supply lines figured out.) But nourishment counted for nothing against the sharpness of my tone when I told them No, they *couldn't* come into the kitchen with sand on their feet while I was scrubbing the floor for the third time that day. ("Can't you do *anything* about that awful floor?" Kitty asked me, early on. "No," I answered. "You might try washing it," she said with a hoarse laugh. "I washed it twice this morning," I told her. "Well wash it again," she said.) The girls were forever reporting instances of my evil nature to Kitty, who cornered me whenever she could and harangued me about how roughly I handled these fragile adolescent blooms, and how badly I was raising my own children.

My own children were aggrieved, not because they were being so badly raised, but because they wanted to get back into their own beds.

George, our willful and venerable tomcat, was aggrieved because he couldn't take his afternoon nap in the sink in the boys' bathroom; and because the one time he did, Robert ran hot water on him. Robert was aggrieved because Gibney and I acted as if we owned the place, and because we treated him as an equal, not as God Almighty. (I doubt if he had any friends, only idolaters or enemies.) Far more self-contained and devious than his wife, he didn't express his outrage openly. When offended, he would soon work in some reference to the far grander places where he had been given warmer welcomes in the past. He told us several times (usually after Gibney had advised him to shut up for Christ's sake and let him get on with his crossword puzzle) about a visit he'd paid to the King of Belgians. The King had a consort or something named Liane who was, Robert said, "not entirely unlike Nancy." ("That bitch. I couldn't stand her," Kitty put in.) One night when the power failed and I was washing the multitudinous dishes by candle light, Robert scuttled into the kitchen with the sideways gait of a crab, and whispered, "Kitty doesn't like to mention it again, but she isn't happy that the dishes aren't more adequately rinsed. Perhaps it might not be inappropriate to rinse them under running water?"

"Perhaps," I agreed. "But we're not going to *have* any running water unless you kids stop flushing the toilets so much."

He puffed hard at his pipe. Then, very mildly, he remarked, "Nancy, in profile and in this poor light, you rather resemble a former hostess of mine, the Queen of Greece." He smirked and left, confident that he had put me in my place, and that place not a palace.

My minor grievances were many, but so funny that I didn't really mind them. My major grievance was my lack of sleep. This was partly due to the vile discomfort of my pad on the terrace floor, but mostly to the Oppenheimer insomnia and seizures, to which I was an unwilling witness.

During the day, they kept the doors to "their room" closed, perhaps to discourage entrance by cats and baby, perhaps to deter me from snooping into their mail, although their habit of flushing this down the toilet, with dire effects on the plumbing, should have been enough to thwart me in such ambitions. Several times they forgot and left a door open when they went out somewhere. On their return, the dialogue was always the same. Kitty (in wild alarm): "Robert! That door's open! We left it shut!" Robert (in tones of the gentlest, gravest suspicion): "It *may* have been an accident."

At night, they opened their doors for maximum ventilation and I, on my bed of nails outside their room, had to hear every word they said (most of them directed against me), every shriek that Kitty emitted in the course of one of her excruciating "pancreas attacks," every howl and groan attendant to Robert's frequent nightmares. Crashes of breaking glass and the smell of smoldering linen also kept me wakeful: they were great believers in drinking and smoking in bed. The first night they were in my residence, I coughed stagily to show them that I could hear them. "My God! She's trying to eavesdrop!" Kitty said. The next morning, I explained the trick acoustics of our stone house, a sounding box where the slightest noise carries unless the doors are closed. "So please close your doors onto the terrace at night," I said. "I sleep out there and I can't help hearing you." They never asked why I slept on the terrace; no doubt they thought that pad was one of my kinks. And they never closed their doors at night.

On rare occasions when I was asleep, Kitty often woke me by shining a flashlight in my face asking why I didn't like her; or by banging around in the kitchen getting ice. All that ice seemed to have a most unfavorable effect on her pancreas. The more ice she got as the night wore on the more subject she was to violent attacks. Along toward dawn, things would quiet down; but along toward dawn was when I had to get up and start on my day's labor. The Oppenheimers awoke refreshed toward noon, when all my early work had been canceled by subsequent inroads and the house was a shambles again. One morning, Kitty rose early to go to St. Thomas and caught me in the act of sweeping the living room. "Well, you're really making an effort today. What happened?" she said approvingly.

Gibney had fewer grievances than the rest of us. He was not a displaced person: he occupied his own bed, in his own foul room at the back of the house and slept well, insulated from the *nachtmusik*. During the day he could retreat to the gatehouse, crammed to the rafters with the wherewithal of his manifold arts and crafts. His dinner appeared on time, and though he often had to share it with the Oppenheimers, he rather enjoyed talking to Robert, whom he baited, and bested, at least from his point of view.

Despite their physical difference — Gibney was tall, heavy, handsome, immensely strong — he and Robert had similarities. They were both leavened Germans: Robert made more supple by his Jewish blood, Gibney more witty by his shot of Irish. Both showed marked symptoms of paranoid megalomania. Both had set up shop as Universal Men, or rather, Universal One-Upsmen. Both were linguists; both loaded with recondite information acquired for display. Robert had a much better memory than Gibney; Gibney much more imagination than Robert. They had many a heated argument, which each thought he'd won hands down.

Gibney wouldn't have done so well if Robert had stuck to atomic physics, but Robert fancied himself a verbalist, and there he was on trembling ground. That summer he had been asked to write an abstruse article for THINK, a publication put out by IBM. He wrote it with great pains, rewrote it, revised the revision, polished that up. Then, pleased as Punch with his production, he proceeded to show it around. He showed it to Kitty, who thought it was marvelous. He showed it to me; I couldn't understand one word of it, although I read every word of it four times. He showed it to Gibney, who said, "Obscurity is no guarantee of profundity" and refrained from further comment. He showed it to the girls.

Then he dispatched it to THINK.

A couple of weeks later, THINK's editor wrote to him: "Dear Dr. Oppenheimer: We were much interested in the first draft of your article," going on to suggest total reorganization and clarification. Robert was the crossest man I have ever seen. I thought his pipe would blow up.

That same mail brought me a gorgeous check from *Redbook* for a story I'd shown to no one but my agent. I didn't mention this around the house; things were bad enough. They got worse when I shot $675 of my new wealth on an enormous electric refrigerator. Even Gibney admitted that this trip was necessary: our food was rotting in the kerosene refrigerator, not because our guests had much food that needed cooling, but because Kitty inserted whole cases of beer at a time, despite my frantic protest, and because she required all that nocturnal ice.

Kitty went to St. Thomas to help Gibney select the new model (she specified the most expensive one) and to supervise his struggles bringing it back. On their way, they stopped off at *Pueblo*, the St. Thomas supermarket, and both bought vast amounts of perishable food. When at last this magnificent machine was installed in our kitchen and actually getting cold, Kitty proceeded to fill it with her purchases, giving me helpful hints on refrigerator care and cleaning as she did so. No doubt she felt especially virtuous because she had finally managed to latch on to plentiful supplies. Soon every slot for eggs was filled with an Oppenheimer egg, the vegetable bin (called a "Misty Crisper" — "Take it back," I told Gibney) filled to the brim with Oppenheimer vegetables, the meat locker with Oppenheimer meat, the commodious shelves with Oppenheimer bread and beer. "There!" Kitty finally said, slamming the door with much satisfaction on a job well done.

I had watched this performance goggle-eyed. Now I asked, "Where would you suggest that I put *our* food?" The kitchen steps were impassable, blocked by dozens of boxes of stuff that Gibney had bought, spoiling fast.

"Oh my God," she said. "You're going to want to *share* it. Well. *Try* not to mess it up too much.

At this I laughed hysterically, and Robert came sidling into the kitchen. He eyed me with suspicion. "Kitty has made a *mot*?"

"*Mot* or less," I told him.

He saw that I was laughing at her, and he was not amused. "Kitty has a delightful wit," he whispered, his volume control at its most vehement low.

In private, Gibney and I tried to analyze Robert's attitude toward his wife. He was certainly no dumbbell: he certainly knew that she was "difficult", often impossible. So why did he never restrain her in her rudeness? Why did he condone, even blandly seem to encourage, her dropping all those bricks? Gibney said it was just another neurotic "test of love," like the excess beer in the icebox and the toilet-flushing: Robert wanted her to be unforgivable, but forgiven for *his* sake. I thought, more simply, that he liked her to be a devil so that he would seem more saintly by contrast. And once or twice, when she said something especially spiteful and Robert sat by in silence, half-smiling, I could have sworn that he was doing a ventriloquist act. He was willing her to be rude, to speak out his own malice for him.

I came to have a sneaking fondness and respect for Kitty, although I took care not to show it. At her worst, she was absolutely without guile, brave as a little lion, and fiercely loyal to her own team.

I can not say as much for Gibney. That summer he played a double game. In private, he complained bitterly to me about the Oppenheimers' encroachments and their paranoid pranks, laying on me the burden of keeping them somewhat in line. But to Kitty and Robert he gave the false impression that he was their friend, and I the family sorehead. They were forever having furtive conferences about my crankiness. Did Gibney think they were doing something wrong? Gibney, the crook, advised them to forget it: it was just my way, to be bossy and nasty.

I was well aware of his treachery and took it as a matter of course. When I needed support, I knew I could count on Gibney to let me down. In this case, of course, he was overjoyed to see my relations with our guests deteriorate. He had never thought Robert was "kind" or "charming"; *he* hadn't wanted to sell them the goddamn land. But quite aside from the pleasures of vindication, Gibney was always pleased to have allies against me;

he had raised the love-hate syndrome to truly rarified heights. One of his reasons for hating me was that I usually didn't act neurotic, and he never felt really cozy except with fellow nuts. "For Christ's sake, the whole thing *is* your fault," he told me when I was imprudent enough to suggest that even he seemed to think I was the prime trouble-maker. "You're the only sane one in this madhouse and it's up to you to keep the peace."

By the first of August I had grave doubts about my own sanity. I felt dizzy and crazed from chronic sleeplessness, and I had lost another ten pounds that I could not afford. But the end was in sight. The Oppenheimers spoke of leaving about the middle of the month.

August 6th, the fourteenth anniversary of the bombing of Hiroshima, was a day of fond nostalgia for our guests, a day of smirks and excitable recall. No one observing Robert Oppenheimer *en famille* that day could question what had been his finest hour. No matter what qualms of conscience Robert later laid claim to — "The scientists have known sin," all that highflown jazz — he transparently *loved* the Bomb and his lordly role in its creation. I think Robert's great problem was that, for all his intelligence, he had no more imagination than a computer.

Kitty's birthday fell on Saturday, August 8th; she'd told me I'd never guess it but she would be forty-nine. In an effort to sweeten my sour image I arranged a little dinner party for that night, inviting Erva Boulon, the former mistress of Trunk Bay, and her new husband Bill Thorp. I had seen Erva a few days before and she had asked, "How are you getting on with them?" "How did *you* ever do it?" I answered. She laughed. "Well. I had the other house to retreat to — they weren't on top of me all the time. And I wasn't taking care of three young children. And I had plenty of help. And I charged them a pretty penny. But *even so*. Believe me, Nancy, you get a medal if you end up on speaking terms."

I got no medal.

Saturday afternoon I was setting the dinner table for eight when Gibney came back from Cruz Bay with the mail. I had a letter from my mother in Boston: my father had died of a stroke four days before. For once, I was glad to be overworked and I got through the evening somehow. Robert had donated champagne for the gala, and the girls got dreadfully drunk. ("It is better for them to get drunk in a loving family milieu," he remarked with much indulgence. I thought it was better for them not to get drunk at all but I kept my mouth shut.)

Knowing full well that Kitty despised my baking ("All that starchy stuff you eat. No wonder you're — " but even she lacked the nerve to complete sentence), I had made a big chocolate cake. I planned to pass it off as a token birthday cake that night and let my children enjoy it thereafter. I didn't have the suitable number of candles so I stuck seven on it. Robert, who knew a square root when he saw one, instantly perceived the strategy of this. "Nancy *knows your age*, Kitty," he hissed. "In her subtle fashion, she is showing you that she *knows your age.*"

I had my own sad reasons for insomnia that night. Sunday morning I went to Caneel Bay and begged for the use of their radiotelephone. I called my mother: she said she didn't need me, but she'd love to see me if I could possibly come.

I went back to Hawksnest and announced that I was splitting for Boston at dawn the next day. This news was well received by everyone except Gibney, who, much as he sometimes hated me, always hated to have me out of sight. I started to dig up some shards of travelling clothes, then stopped to get lunch for my children. There wasn't much left of the birthday leg of lamb. I counted heavily on the cake, which had been scorned as predicted, to fill them up and cheer them up.

When I opened the refrigerator to extract it, it had disappeared. "Don't tell me you've eaten it already," I said to my sons. But they hadn't seen a trace of it. Neither had Gibney nor, presumably the baby.

I went out to the terrace where the Oppenheimers were basking and told them that I had a mystery to solve. The cake had been scarcely touched the evening before, but now it was gone. Had they any theories?

"I gave it to the girls," Kitty said. "They like that sort of glup."

"YOU GAVE IT TO THE GIRLS?"

She bristled. "Well it was *my* cake, wasn't it?"

I hadn't cried before, but now I burst into tears. They dried rapidly when I realized that of all the summer's incidents, this one took the cake.

When I went to "bed" that evening I made a public announcement. I had to be up very early, I faced a difficult day, and I would be very grateful for plenty of silence around the house that night. The Oppenheimers concurred, all muted sympathy.

By midnight, the house lights were still blazing and there was still a lot of strange noise coming from the kitchen. I gave up, got up and went to investigate. Kitty was engaged in an intensive cleaning of the counter-tops.

"Why are you doing that?" I asked her.

"I knew you wouldn't want to go and leave everything so filthy," she explained.

I went back to my pad. By one, the lights were out, the noise had stopped and I was at the edge of that little greased slope down into sleep when the lights went on and more banging came from the kitchen. Kitty had felt the imperative of ice.

I got up and went into the kitchen. "Kitty," I said. "I've *got* to get some sleep. Please, no more lights or noise tonight."

I went back to my pad. Soon there was no *lumiere,* no sound except for the whine of mosquitoes in my ear. But now I was too tired and nervous to sleep. I got up and took an aspirin. I take perhaps one a year, it always makes me sick and I regret it.

Nevertheless, toward three I began to feel drowsy. I should have known better. New clicks and crashes came from the kitchen but only a dim light. Kitty, ever the considerate guest, was getting her ice with the aid of a flashlight this time.

I got up and went into the kitchen. "Kitty," I said in a voice that terrified even me, "no one who drinks all night needs *ice*. You get back in that room and you close the doors and you stay in there if it kills you."

She hit me as hard as she could with her flashlight. She as a weak little woman: the blow was no more than a moth grazing my cheek.

I am a big strong woman. I got a good grip on her shoulder (she felt brittle and light as a katydid) and gave her the bum's rush into "their room" and slammed and barricaded all the doors. Then I went back to my pad, but less than ever to sleep. At five I got up and got breakfast prepared for my children and prepared for take-off.

"When are you coming back, Mama?" they asked.

"When those lunatics go," I told them.

I was sorry to leave the children, but not one bit sorry to leave. I thought I would die in the St. Thomas airport, and again in San Juan, and again at Idlewild. But at eight that night I was in Boston, in a big cool quiet orderly house. My mother took one look at me and said, "Oh, darling. *You* came to take care of *me*?"

Nancy Gibney — who often wrote under the name Nancy Flagg — was a highly respected freelance writer in her day. For a number of years, she was an editor with Vogue magazine in New York. She passed away in 1980. This article originally appeared in a Swiss literary publication in 1970's. The above photograph of Nancy with her two sons John (L) and Ed (R) was taken in June of 1958.

St. John's Steel Unlimited band at the Rockefeller Center 1975

Notes and Quotes from the Kids at the Julius E. Sprauve School

Cultural Flow

I feel lucky to live on St. John. We have green hills and beaches of golden sand. Our waters are crystal clear and full of life. We treat strangers like family and friends. Everybody knows each other by sight. Sadness has no definition and happiness is in everyone's mind. People come here to stay away from worries of all kinds.

Every July is a festive time and there are parades with a special glow and winds with a gentle flow. Tourists come to dine and drink nice wine — to hide themselves from mainland snow.

I feel lucky because of the cultural flow.

Shawn Smith, Sixth Grade

"I am very fortunate to live on St. John, even though I was born on St. Thomas. The people here are caring and forgiving. Many are related, and look out for each other. The tourists come here for the scenery, beaches, and climate — but I am fortunate that I do not have to come to see those things because I already live here.

Julice Harley, Sixth Grade

"St. John's night life is like romancing in a fantasy..!"

Suzette Kelly, Fourth Grade

"Sometimes we have ball games. They are a great deal of fun. Especially the food and beverages. They serve fried chicken and the soda is simply fantastic!"

Eldrina Michel, Fifth Grade

"St. John is the best place to be. There is not a lot of violence."

Jefferson Fessale, Fifth Grade

"I'm proud to live on St. John. We have many trees. On the Fourth of July you can sit or stand in the shade to watch the parade. We have Jam Band music and even Steel Pan groups. Our public bathrooms are clean and decent because many people take care of our little island. All this is about St. John, the little island I live on."

Tiffany Rogers, Fifth Grade

"St. John has a lot of hills that go up and down all the way to town."

Martina Scimeca, Fifth Grade

"St. John is the best place to be because the people care for each other."

Angelique Ramnarine, Fourth Grade

"I think the Virgin Islands are like a dream come true for the fortunate ones like myself. We kind of have a world of our own."

Tiffany Christain, Sixth Grade

"I was born in the Coral Bay Fire Station on November 12, 1981. I would like to tell you about my wonderful island. Our warm turquoise blue water is good for swimming, snorkeling and scuba diving. We have an underwater trail in Trunk Bay and you can watch the fish swim by — mostly in schools, but sometimes just one or two.

You can also go hiking. On the Reef Bay Trail you can see different kinds of plants and trees. Along the way you can see parts of huts that people used to live in, and you can see old Indian writings and symbols.

At Fort Berg, you can see where slaves and soldiers and other people lived long ago.

But St. John isn't just for swimming and hiking — it's for relaxing too. Some nice places to stay are the Hyatt Regency and Caneel Bay Resort. They're stupendous!"

Patricia Blackwood, Sixth Grade

Pappy, the Bionic Creole

by
Gilbert A. Sprauve

Hanging strategically close to the entrance at the top of the steps leading to the gate, is the hand-lettered sign "God's Little Acre". That is where I traveled to for my long-postponed interview with Mr. Albert Sewer. His wife, Pearl, greeted me warmly, a trace of uneasiness visible, since she had expressed her doubts that he could do that kind of thing any more.

To most of us he's known as "Pappy." It's easy for those of us who speak the vernacular to imagine a time in his youth when he was called "Mikase [for Make Haste] Albert." For, to compel him to sit still for any length of time is to torture him. Even at the age of eighty plus. And his impatience-driven witticisms even at a funeral is a source of enough snickering to neutralize the sobs of the bereaved and convince even them that the corpse too smiles.

A reasonably accurate portrayal of Albert is hardly possible without reference to a number of lexical peculiarities of our Creole. And such a requirement might only be natural, if the association of "creolization" with adaptability and resourcefulness is a valid one. Thus, Creole terms are used to describe what he is like and what he is not like. His gait, for instance, even in his eighty-second year is not that of a man slingering, or liming, much less doting. It's more like someone cooping or stalking. Not with mischief or any form of malice on his mind. Rather, he appears to be on the watch for a human or practical problem in want of a common sense solution. Can such a man ever truly relax and rest, you have to ask yourself. And you probably answer yourself in the negative if you have known Pappy for a day and know what it is to be caged in on all sides by complacency, resignation and indifference. Yet, how come he is always so pleasant, jovial, never disagreeable, you ask yourself next, falling back on the pronunciation we apply to this English word to make it mean "unpleasant and irritable." Insulation from the ravages of petty narrow-mindedness takes different forms among different people. Some people say, "The circus is passing and the dogs are barking." Albert is likely to mutter simply, "Let the jackass bray!" The stories he relates capture this predilection for brinkmanship and his appreciation for ready, practical solutions.

Take the one about the time of the floating rum. When Pappy asked me if I knew about that time, I assumed he was talking about a time when booze in the islands was so abundant it could be said to be floating. So, what about it? Albert hastened to clarify: "I'm talking about a time when a boat from Demerara or someplace like dat, had sink an' you could fine casks of rum floating all about de Caribbean...Well, dey had dis fellow dey call Brookson. Was livin' on Lovango during the time I was staying over dere with Miss Sewer, de school teacher..."

"Yo tellin' me dey had a school on Lovango?"

"Till de Americans close it, sometime in de twenties or thirties when dey decide it didn' have enough students to keep it open."

"So, wha' Brookson had to do with rum floatin'?"

"Brookson was a man know so much bout fishin' he could stay

on de shore look at de movement o' de water an' tell yo wha' kind o' fish out dere beatin'. Anyway, he rig up a net an' whatnot an' de next t'ing yo know, he catch a whole cask, bring it to shore, an' settle down on it."

"Settle down on it? Yo tellin'me..."

"Drink it off all by heself. Send him stark murder crazy! He walk about the cay throwin' rockstone on de roof o' people house, declarin', 'De boys beatin' de gyurls!'...Till dey had to strap him down, put him on a sailboat to send him St. Thomas. Even den, he mother was dere to stop dem before de boat sail. 'Come, yo li'l sonuvabitch, yo! Come take a drink wid yo mother before yo go 'way!'

"An' wha happen to Brookson?"

"Lovango had a fleet a sailboat didn't make joke. Dey set up a fo'boom, an' in two twos yo lose sight o'dem as dey pass through de passage an' head fo' town. Everyt'ing went to town in dose days. Not Shark Wharf like in later days. Dey had him in de hospital in town for a coup o' days. Pump out he stomach. An' he come back as good as ever. Ah don' know how dey do it, but he come back as good as he was!"

Albert was one of nine children. Was it the Crucian half of his heritage that accounts for his impestuous nature? His father, Lanzy, was a sea captain and boat owner who plied the trade between Coral Bay and St. Croix. "De good t'ing about it is dat you could make it to St. Croix on one tack. And back on one tack too! Dey took cattle, charcoal, baskets, wood for burnin'." And what did they return with. Lanzy, for one, returned with a wife. "A woman who in a fight could butt harder dan any man. W'en she butt a man, he go down!" according to Albert. So much so that whenever his father's mother who lived close by sensed that trouble was brewing between the spouses, she would sing out to her son: "Come up here, Lanzy, before dat Crucian wench kill yo' backside!"

Mrs. Sewer, (nee Joseph on St. Croix), when it was time to orient her brood towards useful careers in life, decided Albert would be the vendor. He could count faster than all the others. So, off she'd pack him with a basket of cocoa and coffee to make his rounds in Coral Bay, John's Folly and the little villages in the area. And who ever saw or knew a successful itinerant vendor who didn't have a quick mind and wasn't adept at wordplay?

So gifted was Albert in this area, in fact, that in his boyhood years with the Moravian Church, as a helper and groom the ministers tried to "rope [him] in" for a career in the Ministry. Never, even then, one to stand still that long, Albert instead learned all there was to learn about the game of cricket from Pastor Osborne, from Antigua, he believes, all about spin bowling and leg break. "Reverend Osborne had the island properly organized with cricket teams: a team in Coral Bay, one in East End, one in Mary's Point, another in Bordeaux and so on." No doubt Albert had in mind to somehow emulate his mentor's contribution, when after returning to the islands after years in New York City, he joined with many of the Eastern Caribbeaners and revived cricket on the islands. The transition was easy, since he had played cricket with their kinfolk in places like Van Courtland Park while in the City. They confer on him even today boundless esteem and affection for rehabilitating their national sport in the Virgin Islands and integrating them better into our society through it.

While in New York as a young man, where he'd been lured by two older siblings, he gained the rank of insider of sorts in the Garment District. He started out as a sweeper as he recalls. In short order he'd climbed the ladder to the ranking of entrepreneur. He credits free night school classes with the quick progress. One has the impression that the quick learner in him and his innate skills and talent must have been in constant rebellion against the strictures and pacing of the classroom. "Enough of that. That's stale stuff. Let's move on to another chapter!" You can just hear him addressing the class and its instructor. The ironies of his Garment District experience are intriguing . In fact, they are what make him the enigma that he is to many. Take the stockpile of insider one-liners constantly at the tip of his tongue developed by the ethnic majority of the District. At weddings and other social events when Albert is called to the mike (which he invariably approached in the past with flute in hand) to offer a toast or two, you might see one or two of the locals shuffle nervously or break out in a cold sweat. It's not for fear of his off-color jokes, as some might claim. Since he is ultimately a man of taste. Rather, it's anxiety that he might offend one of the visitors, not prepared to have him spill the beans on how others have stereotyped those like themselves and those who are unlike them.

Ask Albert about Alstein and he chuckles. Alstein faced the Saints Peter and Paul Catholic Church in downtown Charlotte Amalie. You could enter the small establishment in tatters and emerge looking like a million bucks. It was Albert's clever way of sort of turning the tables on the Garment District experience while turning a neat buck for himself. "A Jew that I worked for in the City had a last name that ended with the syllable "stein". He died, and his widow made me the foreman of his factory. So, when I came out and started my business in St. Thomas I decided to call it "Alstein". People used to come off the ship and head straight to my place. And they would look to fight with me too!"

"Fight wid yo? But, for what?"

"'Where's Mr. Alstein?', they would ask. 'Why you need to see Mr. Alstein?' I would answer. 'Never mind that! Just get me Mr. Alstein!' the customer would say, losing his temper. 'You're looking at him!'"

The quintessential Creole experience? Perhaps, unless you opt for the following incident that Pappy relates when asked to recount that singular experience that he feels he will never forget:

"Dat's easy! Captain John Henry had a boat he used to sail with passengers and cargo to Coral Bay. He had a dummy son. Strong like a ox. When it was time for boardin' de ladies on de boat it was his job to lift dem up on de beach and set dem down on de boat. So dey don' get dey clothes wet. One day he was heading to Coral Bay. When we reach Rams Head de sea was when I tell yo rough, I mean ROUGH. Had de boat pitchin' an' tossin'. All of a sudden, de dummy look at he father at de helm, sing out something like 'Hnnya, Pyyaapyaa!' Jump up from where he was sittin' 'gainst de mass. Went at he father. Haul him off de tiller. Take de tiller and steer de boat out into de deep water. We find it calm out dere and complete de trip! Who say dummy ain' got no sense???"

Albert is first and foremost a practical man. Next, you might say, he's a community minded citizen. As such, once he'd firmly re-planted his feet on the home soil, his agenda was to find and demonstrate solutions to what he saw as backwardness and stagnation at home, though he would never label the problems as such. On the day of Herman Sprauve's funeral, in the midst of a conversation over a drink at Fred's that started with Albert confidentially poking fun at the white hair on a Black man's head that he said favored a salt pond with ripe salt and ended with Albert and the same man reminiscing about old-time cricketeers, Albert give his analysis of the socio-economic and to some extent the socio-political dilemma of Virgin Islanders.

"There are a lot of people around here that learned to do several things and do each one of them well. Which is all well an' good. Except for, it makes a problem trying to get people to cooperate. Our people tend to be independent because of this. I had to travel to New York and work with the Jews down in the Garment District to learn how you divide the tasks and everybody prospers."

Traditions at home don't die easily. And Albert is the proverbial rolling stone. Constantly on the move and bubbling with practical ideas from the world outside. How do they mesh, Albert and his people? From this corner, we would say his pragmatism prevails and he is holding his own. "Yo cyan' do anyt'hing alone," he insists. "I get dat from de Jews. Yo have to have cooperation. Yo have to have confidence and trust. Once yo understan' if you gain I gain, yo could work together. Now, w'en I was a young fellow an' a man got a pasture to clear, an' he hol' club, yo didn' have to call people to work fo yo. De word get out. A gang come from Bordeaux an' another one come from Saint Quaco. De quantity o' work w'a dey would do in one day, a man couldn' pay dem to do. De man dem come wid cutlass sharpen on both side. W'en dey swing it forward it chop, an' on de backswing it chop again. All de time dey determined dat dem Bordeaux boys or de Southside boys, or whoever, ain' going' cut mo' bush dan dem. Jus' make sure yo have food an' drink fo dem. Da's all it take — an' de determination dat no gang could work harder dan deres own!" Mrs. Sewer spoke up at this point, saying a similar institution existed on her home island.

When the time has been ripe he has engaged in political organizing. As was the case in the campaigns to put the late Cyril E. King in Government House, the second of which was spectacularly successful. "Yo have to organize de people!" he insists. He got elected to the Board of Education where he advocated an industry in school uniform manufacturing that would at the same time teach a useful vocational trade and generate jobs for the young. He attends the Moravian Church regularly and serves on any committee where people are looking for able-bodied, progressive thinkers and doers. But mostly, doers! When they get to thinking matters out and they delay too long they look up from their deep thoughts and wonder where Pappy disappeared to.

Dr. Gilbert A. Sprauve of St. John is a Dutch and English Creole scholar and Professor of Modern Languages at the University of the Virgin Islands. He received his Pd.D. in linguistics from Princeton University. He speaks fluent French, and is active in a wide range of community affairs.

More About Les

by
Cap'n Fatty Goodlander

Passion. That's the key. That's the single element which runs through artist Les Anderson's life. He's a passionate, lustful man — a man of enormous appetites.

His knurled hands tell the story; they do not look like the hands of a sensitive painter. Instead, they look like the hands of a boxer, or a commercial fishermen, or a rodeo cowboy. They are the hands of a man who has grabbed at life, held it by the throat, and kissed it full on the lips. A hedonist. A lover of life. A bon vivant.

The second most important thing to understand about Les is that he is *driven* to create. He has no option. He must paint. Or wither.

The final thread that runs through the fabric of Les's life is more delicate but just as important. Les is an extremely romantic man. He's enthralled by the women in his life. At each of his private crossroads stands a Women of Importance. He still believes in True Love. Happy Endings. And All the Rest.

"My father was Les 'Carrot Top' Anderson," said Les Anderson. "He played country and western music. I never really knew him. He left home when I was just a baby. We were living in California by then. But I saw him on TV a couple of times, playing with Bob Wills. I guess you could say my mother was the central figure in my life."

Les Anderson was born in 1944 in Tulsa, Oklahoma. His mother, Mannette Bock, was an artist by profession and temperament. She worked for *Walt Disney Studios*, and was involved in such prestigious projects as the animated feature film *Fantasia*. "Her specialty was air-brushing in special effects," said Les. "She didn't have any formal training as an artist, yet she managed to do quite well."

She was also a hard worker who was intent on providing Les and his younger brother, David, with a stable home. She saved their pennies, put in long hours, and moonlighted at other artistic endeavors. "Often, she wouldn't get home until after we were asleep. I'd cook for my brother. Around 1955, she'd managed to save up enough money to put a small down payment on a modest house. She is quite a women. I have a lot of respect for her."

Some young men wonder what they will do when they grow up. They struggle to pick a profession worthy of a lifetime. Not Les. "From my very first memory, I knew I wanted to be an artist. It has always been *the* central motivating fact of my existence. There's art, and then there is the rest of my life. Almost everything I do is affected by the fact that I'm an artist."

In conjunction with being an artist, Les was fascinated by anything mechanical. He enjoyed figuring out how things went together — how they moved. He loved to work with his hands — to rebuild engines, fix cars, repair appliances, design refrigeration systems, and build almost anything. As a young man he almost instinctively seemed to understand how to weld, braze, and burn metal.

Woodworking also intrigued him. "I can't imagine not spending the majority of my time painting, but if I couldn't — I'd love to own a good junk yard. That would be fun. I'd spend all day creating huge outdoor metal sculptures."

Les enjoys life. He has a boyish enthusiasm for having fun. Like many creative artists, he is somewhat of a glutton at the table of life. His interests are extremely diverse, yet his focus remains quite narrow. In some ways he is like the dished mirrors of a telescope — reducing the whole of a dark universe to a sliver of light upon his canvas. This is what makes artists so interesting. So noble. And often, so unhappy.

Les is often very highly focused. He lives almost totally within the moment. If he is driving along a highway, and the setting sun warmly illuminates a tree in a particularly intriguing way — Les stops his car.

Only the horns behind him remind him to pull off the road.

Yet he has a practical, down-to-earth side. "I wanted to earn my living by drawing, so I got a degree in technical illustrating. I learned to draw some very nice airplane parts. Unfortunately, just about the time I received the degree, I realized I wasn't going to use it."

"It was obvious to me even back then that the future in technical illustration was in the computing field. I didn't want to be a CAD operator, I wanted to be an artist.

"At one point, I attempted to enlist in the French Foreign Legion," Les said matter-of-factly. "I thought I had just the right temperament for those boys. But, much to my amazement, they rejected me."

Les joined the Navy, and soon found himself in Vietnam, running a Swift patrol boat. It's the only period in his life he seemed somewhat reluctant to discuss. He admits he was forever changed by the experience. "I had a boat very similar to the smallest St. John ferry boat — the one named the Nicky V. Above the pilot house was a giant machine gun. It was very fast. We had mortars aft. The whole boat bristled with weaponry. But we had absolutely no armor — no protection from incoming rounds. We often got shot up, and sometimes we got hit without even knowing it. It was a strange experience. There was a lot in the movie *Apocalypse Now* which people don't believe — but a lot of it was real. I mean, we used to water ski behind our boat."

While Les was in 'Nam, his mother, Mannette, developed an interest in scuba diving. She joined a diving club and fell in love with a man named Desoto Bock.

He was a sailor, and they left California in a 40' carvel planked Newporter ketch named *Restless*. They cruised Mexico, banged a left at the Panama Canal, and finally grew tired of cruising when they reached St. John, USVI.

Les Anderson, fresh out of the Navy, returned to California. He got a job as a refrigeration mechanic. But he wasn't happy. He wanted more out of life — much more. So when his mother wrote about how wonderful the sleepy little island of St. John was, Les decided to visit.

"I left my car — actually the Bank of America's car — parked right outside the Bank of America. I left a note underneath its wiper telling 'em good bye. At least they didn't have to hunt for it. I never looked back. That was over 20 years ago.

"The moment I arrived in St. John, I fell in love with the place," said Les. "It was so beautiful. Everywhere I looked there were tropical scenes I wanted to paint. Again and again I was struck by the beauty of the island. Arriving here was so exciting; living on St. John back in the 1960s was such an adventure. I loved the people; was fascinated by the local customs and attitudes. I knew immediately I wanted to stay. Hell, the sailing was good, the island picture-perfect, and a bottle of rum cost less than a buck. It sure seemed like Paradise to me."

He got a job as a diesel mechanic at *Antilles Boat Yard* in St. Thomas. He saved his money, purchased a 25' Gaff Cutter named *Banshee*, and moved to Coral Bay.

"Those were wonderful days. I met Peter and Dorothy Muilenburg, Andy and Janet Rutnik, Jerry and Christine Singer, the Gibneys and the Marshes, Vie Kendell..." said Les. "The road from Cruz Bay to Coral Bay often wasn't open, and we used a 13' Boston Whaler for transportation. Coral Bay was quiet then. I'd paint all week, and then sell the paintings to tourists in St. Thomas on the weekends. A lot of my stuff wasn't very good back then, but then again, there wasn't a lot of competition, either. I was happy. I was making my living selling my art. It didn't bother me that I could barely afford rice, beans, and lentils. That was enough."

Les got more and more interested in cruising under sail. Even though the *Banshee* was in rather rough shape, he took off down island. "I used to have to sleep with my arm over the bunk so the boat wouldn't sink in the middle of the night. I spent a number of years in St. Barts hanging out with Lou Lou Magras and the boys, and toured the entire Lesser Antilles."

While Les was in Martinque, French West Indies, he met St. John sailor Augie Holland on the cowhorn *Taurus* (now *Sea Chantey*, ex *Sealegs*). He told Les about a friend who was going to build a boat — but finally decided not to. There was a pile of lumber and a 55 gallon drum of glue on Hassel Island. It was for sale for two hundred bucks.

Les returned to the Virgin Islands, and purchased the pile of lumber. He began to construct his dream boat with his own hands. He shaped her by ax, adze, auger, drawspoke, and handsaw. It took him two years of solid effort.

But it was worth it. The result was a 36' gaff-rigged engineless schooner named *Penelope* whose design was based on the lovely old Block Island schooners of New England.

It was immediately apparent that she was a fast, practical vessel. But she was also more than that — like everything Les does, she was a work of art.

From the dashing rake of her lofty spars to the graceful line of her pronounced sheer, she looked like a magic vessel which had just sailed out of a romantic painting.

By this time, Les was becoming more and more of a respected artist. The launching of *Penelope* was a turning point. He was turning his larger-than-life dreams into solid reality. He no longer seemed bound by the past. The future was full of promise. All caution was thrown to the winds; all restraint went out the porthole. His paintings were suddenly selling for higher and higher fees. His fame was spreading. He was an Artist with a capital "A."

And, of course, he had style. Particularly in the French West Indies, he was widely beloved. St. Barts was enthralled by him. He was an "Artist" in very aspect of his life. His laughter was a braying bark — without the slightest tempering. He was not known for his diplomacy. He had strong opinions, sharp tastes, and definite views. He didn't care whether people loved him or not. Not in the slightest. So what? Who cares? His life was a headlong rush toward the next *color*, *shape*, and *emotion*.

He was, yes indeed, an Artist. "More rum!" he'd shout.

The gentle shyness of his inner personality combined strangely with his harsh outspokenness. There was much to love about the man within this period of artistic flowering — and plenty to not, too.

In the end, he was Himself. A personal creation. The Caribbean Sea Gypsy as Painter Extraordinaire! Take 'em, or leave 'em. You had to deal with Les on his terms back then.

Most loved him.

"He was a difficult man to know; but well worth the effort," said a friend. True.

He had a certain Presence. When he walked into a room, his body/soul/energy defined the space around him. He dominated it. He was already somebody — even when he was nobody. There was a certain energy — a creative aura which swirled about him. The other people and objects within the same room always seemed to exist within their relationship to him.

It was as if there was an invisible spotlight — sometimes wonderfully benign, sometimes horribly cruel — which followed Les around.

The stories about him were legendary. When one of his teeth got knocked out, he nonchalantly carved a replacement out of Lignum Vitae wood.

Once, he made the mistake of selling a painting he wasn't perfectly satisfied with. It haunted him. After a while, he visited the new owner, ripped the painting out of its frame, and started furiously dabbing new colors onto it — until the new owner and Les got into a *serious* tug-a-war... yanking the work back and forth....the owner screaming about ownership, and Les screaming about the Rights of an Artist...

When he busted up all of his ribs, he duct-taped his body back together long enough to sail to Jost Van Dyke, and win at Foxy's

Wooden Boat Regatta.

He opened Wet Willy's bar on St. Thomas and scared many a drunk stone-sober by wiring up a dead pelican to move its jaw realistically as it "spoke" (via hidden a intercom) from the other side of the grave.

He once reportedly rebuilt a jeep engine by the side of the road with only a sledge hammer, pry bar, and yard stick for tools.

His was a magic life filled with bright rainbows, warm golden showers and floating flowers descending from both heaven and hell.

The only problem was that Les began to burn a little too brightly. This often happens with people driven to create. His candle not only was aflame at both ends; it was "nuclear" on the sides, middle, center, etc. His hands shook. His eyes were redder than a stop sign.

He was observed lurching down the street of Cruz Bay more and more often. His friends began to worry. Les seemed intent on drinking himself into an early grave. Local investors started quietly buying up his paintings — secure in the knowledge that their value would increase dramatically upon his death.

It was that serious. An old familiar story. Some people burn so fiercely that they seek to drown themselves in strong fermented liquids. They usually accomplish their goal.

Enter Mary Blazine. She came to St. John to visit her friend Cheryl Miller.

Mary is also an artist — but of a different sort. When she's not sculpturally "making things" out of roots and vines and such, she's using a Xerox machine as her canvas and brush. She's far more modern and hip than Les; she could be equally at home in the New York, Japan, or LA art circles.

She is a strikingly handsome woman. There is a certain classic Old World grace in her body movements; the way she walks, how she turns her head. There is also the slight arrogance of the artist; she knows what she likes, wants, and desires.

She desired Les.

When St. John society realized that Les and Mary were becoming a "unit" — many were horrified. It seemed a clear case of Beauty and the Beast. The Old Maid's Club (misery loves company) took her aside, and warned her about Les's reputation in their strongest terms. She ignored them with an indulgent smile.

Mary seemed to be skipping down the streets of Cruz Bay in happiness. Seldom has a women appeared so enlivened by love. Les stopped shaking; started opening up more paint cans than rum bottles.

Les and Mary announced they would marry — more or less. The wedding was to take place June 8th, 1991 on Jost Van Dyke, a small island just north of St. John. The famous Foxy Callwood of Jost would be the Best Man. The word quickly went up and down the coconut telegraph; this was definitely going to be one of the social events of the season.

Unfortunately, as the first of the hundreds of invited guests arrived, they were horrified to hear someone say, "Mary's dead."

At first they thought it was the sickest, most disgusting joke they'd ever heard... but soon realized the actual truth of the matter.

A woman named Mary Margarita Callwood of Jost had died. She had been known to many Caribbean sailors as Fire Breathing Mary because she... well, she breathed fire whenever the mood struck her. She loved to dance, and had corralled many a sailor into sharing a few reggae-induced tussles on the dance floor. She enjoyed the Jump-Ups, especially New Year's Eve and Foxy's Wooden Boat Regatta. If she wanted more room on the dance floor, she'd take a swig out of her bottle, flick her Bic, and shoot a ten foot long bright orange flame out her mouth.

That usually did the trick.

Anyway Fire Breathing Mary was truly dead, and her funeral was scheduled for 1 pm in the only church on the island.

Which was the same exact church in which a hundred people were now just arriving as scheduled (also exactly at 1pm) to attend a different Mary's church wedding... not this Mary's church funeral.

However, God had rescheduled things His way. After all, this is the Caribbean. Strange things like this seem to happen with disconcerting regularity. The situation was curious, but no one's fault. Who are we mere mortals to argue with Him and His plans?

Everyone decided to have the wedding down the beach at Foxy's Bar instead of the church. This turned out to be a good idea. Mary had actually expired on Tortola, and her ferry back to Jost was running a little slow. In true West Indian tradition, Mary was late for her own funeral.

But the situation was, indeed, a strange one. On the east end of the beach was a crowd of gaily dressed people weeping tears of joy at Mary's wedding.

At the same time, over at the west end of the same beach, a crowd of somber people in black clothes wept tears of sorrow.

There were odd moments where the two groups occasionally overlapped. "This is Mary's lucky day!" didn't strike everyone on Jost in quite the same way. "Do you think it will last?" was equally sick.

A group of Les's friends quietly discussed the dreaded possibility of Les showing up late for his own wedding... and being the nervous over-excited groom, not understanding why they were foolishly attempting to stop him from joining his Mary inside... Les fighting his way into the church.... (Such a rude shock might induce a heart attack. *His* tombstone, thus, might read, "Les in No More!")

"God," somebody said following a similar line of reasoning, "we've *got* to make sure that Les ends up leaving with the *right* Mary."

Despite a rather disconcerting beginning, the actual wedding went smoothly.

A large circle of flowers and friends and family was formed around Les and Mary on the beach at Foxy's. Poems were read, songs sung, and rings exchanged. Smoking herbs wafted over the crowd to drive away evil spirits. Symbols of earth, heaven, nature, and the sea were brought forth.

Four young beautiful flower girls danced throughout the moving ceremony. They danced like Spirit Nymphs of Love, and showered the crowd of people encircling Les and Mary and Foxy and Shirley Reid with fresh cut blossoms.

The circle of friends and family and lovers recited reverently Sophocles' *Power of Love*, which begins...

> My children, know Love is not Love alone,
> But in her name lie many names concealed:
> For she is death, imperishable force,

Desire unmixed, wild Frenzy, Lamentation;
In her are summed all impulses that drive
To Violence, Energy, Tranquillity....

Foxy couldn't resist; his impromptu speech after the poem brought gales of loving laughter to the crowd.

A huge cheer went up: Les and Mary were married. "Let the party begin!" yelled Foxy, and it did. Big time.

The following year was a particularly good one for Les. He stopped drinking, and once again his art took center stage in his life. Within the stability of his new marriage, he was suddenly very productive.

He attended a record number of shows, and his sales were good. And, since he was a sailor, he saved his money to take a cruise down-island in his schooner.

Unfortunately, while attending the St. Barts Regatta in 1992, he almost died from acute appendicitis. He had to be rushed to the airport, and air-ambulanced to Guadeloupe — where doctors were standing by to operate within minutes of his arrival.

Les not only survived the painful ordeal, but he made a full, if slow, recovery. But he'd scented his own death. That is bound to have a lasting effect on an individual — especially an artist. Suddenly, he was even more committed to making sure he found the time to paint.

During his recovery, Les and Mary decided to build a modest house on a small parcel of property they own on the East End of St. John.

Les immediately began to turn that dream into reality, and, of course, the result was one of the more unusual homes on St. John. Even the cement in the foundation was pigmented to look similar to the old cement used in St. John in the early 1900s. Numerous old ballast stones (brought from Europe on sailing cargo ships as ballast, and discarded so the ships could return homeward filled with molasses and rum) were used, and Les has an interesting story about each.

A local carpenter who occasionally helped Les out during the construction of the house said it was a wonderful learning experience — as soon as he stopped bringing his square, level, and plumb-bob to the site.

What's next? "Perhaps a gallery," said Les. "Now that the house and studio are finished, that might be the next step. I'd like to have a gallery which would feature my paintings continuously — not just a week or so at a time. And, of course, we'd sell other things — but not tourist junk."

As always, Les's life revolves around his art. Many aspects of modern society do not concern him. When questioned about his personal feelings concerning local politics, he said, "The island is beautiful. I like the people. But I know nothing of politics. It does not concern me. I am an artist."

Herman Emanuel Sprauve

by Delita Sprauve Roberts

September 7, 1926 - December 9, 1992

"Grace be unto you, and peace, from God our Father, and the Lord Jesus Christ." *I Corinthians 1:3*

Herman Emanuel Sprauve was born to Diana Elizabeth Fleming and Julius Sprauve on September 7, 1926 in Estate Sieben, Mandahl, St. John, Virgin Islands, the second child and only son of his mother and fourth child of his father.

Because he was the only son, he was treated special by his aunts and uncles.

Herman was christened and confirmed in the Nazareth Lutheran

Church in St. John. As a young boy, Herman attended the then Bethany School in Pastory, St. John. He walked miles to school and at times rode a donkey or horse. When the journey got tiresome, he would stay with relatives living in Sieben and return the following day. Because of a fear of the sea, his mother did not allow him to travel across the water to attend high school in St. Thomas. Besides Estate Mandahl and Sieben, Herman lived in Sesmon Hill (Gift Hill), Grunwaldt and subsequently moved to Pine Piece with his mother and stepfather.

After completing the Bethany School, Herman worked several jobs. He worked at the Conservation Corp, the Deep Sea Fishing Company, Caneel Bay Plantation, the contracting company building Caneel Bay, and the Public Works Department. He also skippered the Government boat (1958) for the St. John Administrator's office, and in the early 1960's he worked for the VI National Park.

He drove the first GMC jeep in St. John. The vehicle belonged to the Department of Public Works and was used to transport food, supplies and equipment to the Cruz Bay, Coral Bay and John's Folly schools on St. John.

Herman was joined in matrimony to Blanche Smith. Their union brought nine children, five boys and four girls. In later years, Herman married Delma R. Callwood. They were blessed with one boy and one girl.

A self-taught musical genius, Herman inspired many with his talents and thrilled his audiences with his saxophone playing and beautiful, melodious operatic voice. He also played the maracas and other instruments. Herman and his band played, to the delight of audiences, for dances in the American and British Virgin Islands. Herman delighted the neighbors in Pine Piece when he practiced and sang. His special musical ability was bestowed on his children. Herman loved and admired music legends such as Nat King Cole, Hank Williams, Eddie Arnold and Roger Whitaker. One of his favorite hymns was "Precious Lord, Take My Hand."

Herman had a great sense of humor. Many were entertained by the stories he told. One of these was about a large dog which he referred to as "Bison," and about how it chased him one night while walking from Mandahl. According to Herman, Bison chased him into a tank of water where, he claimed, he stayed for four hours.

While working for a Puerto Rican company, Herman learned Spanish and spoke it fluently. He loved people, all races, colors and creeds. Some visitors who traveled to our pristine Virgin islands remain his personal friends to this day. This was attested to by the tremendous number of calls, letters and get-well wishes when he was ill. He was charming and possessed charisma. He smiled with people and received them with open arms.

Herman appreciated people so much that when he was assigned a doctor, he told us that he got the prettiest doctor on the St. Thomas Hospital staff. The registered nurses of the Intensive Care Unit spoiled and pampered him. They looked out for his welfare and provided quality care to him.

Given the miracle of life, Herman thoroughly enjoyed it and lived it to the fullest. His favorite pastime was reading, a daily habit. Louis L'Amour, author of western novels, was his favorite. He traded novels with his friends and relatives. Herman kept the Bible on his bed and read passages nightly. Herman loved the sea, fishing and trap fishing, and captained his own boat.

Herman traveled extensively throughout the Caribbean islands where he met many friends. When visiting Tortola and Virgin Gorda, his favorite Caribbean islands, he would stop and serenade his friends along the way, and they looked forward to his yearly visits. He loved those islands and their people. But most of all, he loved St. John. While he made visits to other places, he remained a permanent life-long citizen of St. John. He was part of the place.

A self-employed businessman, Herman owned and operated Herman E. Sprauve Taxi Bus Service, a bright canary-yellow safari bus. He was a careful and safe driver who drove with extreme caution with deep concern for the safety of his passengers. He obeyed the law and never had an accident. Herman enjoyed transporting passengers from Cruz Bay, Caneel Bay, Hawksnest, Trunk Bay and Cinnamon Bay on a daily basis. His passengers included the workers from Cinnamon Bay and Caneel Bay Plantation and island visitors. Herman made an invaluable contribution to the St. John community and the hospitality industry.

Herman took ill in October, 1992 and was admitted to the St.

Thomas Hospital. He spent one week on the medical ward and was subsequently transferred to the Intensive Care Unit. Herman Emanuel Sprauve accepted Christ as his personal Savior. Even though he was unable to speak because of tubes in his throat he groaned or nodded his head in a "yes" manner to indicate the acceptance of God. He assured us that he asked God for forgiveness and for eternal blessings from the Almighty. He died on Wednesday, December 9, 1992 at approximately 4:40am. He took his last breath after relatives arrived and touched him.

Relatives, friends and the community all mourned his passing. We rest assured that he has departed to a better place where he will feel no pain or suffering.

Herman loved life, he lived life and he enjoyed life! His was a colorful one. The man who possessed a great kindness and compassion for mankind has departed this life and gone to a higher and better life, to rest in the arms of the Almighty.

We will remember his endearing smile, his endearing personality, his warmth, and his kindness.

"The Lord lift up His countenance upon thee, and give thee peace."
Isaiah 41:10

Herman Sprauve is survived by his wife Delma; his daughters Diana, Delita, Clarice, Sonia, Nealia, and Eulalie; his sons Herman Jr., Edwin, Glen, David, and Neal: his brothers Hilton, Kenneth, Julius, Elroy, Vernon, and Liston; his sisters Clarissa Francis, Leona George, Rhynita Thomas, Joan Ricci, and Idalia Varlack; his aunts Dena Thomas and Elaine Sprauve; and his uncle David Fleming. (Herman's brother Roy is deceased.) At the time of

Herman's death, he had 43 grandchildren and 11 great grandchildren.

The author of the above piece, Delita Sprauve Roberts, is one of Herman's daughters. She was born at home in the Pine Piece area of St. John in December of 1948. She attended Julius E. Sprauve School in Cruz Bay and then the Charlotte Amalie High School on St. Thomas. After attending the College of the Virgin Island (now UVI), she moved to Washington, D.C, where she worked for the National Science Foundation. In 1986 she graduated from the University of the District of Columbia with a degree in Public Administration. Returning to the VI in June of 1990, Delita went to work for the VI National Park.

She wishes to especially thank Hilton, Virginia, and Delma Sprauve for their help while researching the above family history. It was originally written for Herman Sprauve's funeral booklet.

The Boulon Legacy

by

Erva A. Denham

The tall bearded strawberry blond man climbs off his motorcycle after the ride from Cruz Bay to Windswept and is greeted first by the screeching of cockatoos and cockatiels, and then by the usual teller of the day's tales, his dog, Schooner. Schoonie is compelled to report the preposterous behavior of the mastiff, Jessica. Meanwhile, Jessie, tail wagging furiously, protests her innocence, as Fish the cat, who nearly trips the cyclist as he affectionately rubs himself against the man's legs, bites his feline tongue to keep from laughing out loud. All of this squalling, barking and tail wagging is augmented with hellos, hugs and kisses from our cyclist's wife, Kimberly, and their two sons, Devon and Revel, each one anxious to claim his attention with stories of the day's events, how Revel made a great catch in today's ball game, how Devon had learned a new piece at steelband practice, and how the groceries had been delivered at Trunk Bay from St. Thomas. The cacophony has its charm - it is music to his ears. It is a normal homecoming after a day's work in St. Thomas where he is a marine biologist with the Division of Fish and Wildlife.

His name Ralf H. Boulon, Jr., but he is better known as Rafe, the nickname he has carried since childhood. The name suits him — it rolls tranquilly off the tongue suggesting the man himself - quiet, peaceful, loving and totally honorable. So what's his story?

Let's go back to the year 1908 and the city of Richmond, Virginia. Frank E. Hartwell has just received his latest set of orders from the U.S. Weather Bureau. His family is excited by the news; this time, he has received a permanent position. By now, packing up and moving on to new environs has become second nature to his wife, Bertha, and their two children. Bertha and Frank met at Oberlin College where they both were students, and were married after graduation. Their three children, Erva, Frank, Jr. (who died of diphtheria in early childhood), and the youngest, Ralf, were born in Ada, Ohio, but the family did not live there for very long. The first major move was to Lincoln, Nebraska where the family experienced their first tornado. They agreed that they could do without another.

In 1898, the United States had won a little skirmish called the Spanish American War, and it wasn't long before the Hartwell family received orders to move to Cienfuegos, Cuba where Frank would be stationed for six months. The family friends in Lincoln all assured them they should pack up all of their winter clothing as they were sure to find that it snowed in Cuba just like it did everywhere else. Frank, the meteorologist, knew better, however, and the winter paraphernalia was left in storage. The trip to Cuba started with a steamboat ride down the Mississippi to New Orleans where they met the freighter that would take them to Havana. On arrival there was the train trip to Cienfuegos, some 150 miles away, as the crow flies. The strongest memory of the trip for both children was the hard, uncomfortable rush-covered seats which they both found to be inordinately scratchy.

Because they were to be in Cuba for less than a year, their quarters were located in a small hotel which gave Bertha considerable freedom, as meals were included as a part of the living expenses. All of this changed, however, when Bertha, looking over the balcony one morning, saw one of the waiters taking a bath in the courtyard below. She was horrified. Not only was the man naked, but he was bathing in one of the restaurant's dish pans. Deciding that this was highly unsanitary, she made other arrangements for the preparation of food. While in Cuba, both children learned to speak Spanish with the help of a young girl who was hired to tutor them. Regular schooling was out of the question, but between the tutor and two college educated parents, the children did not suffer.

The next move was to Key West, Florida where they were fortunate enough to stay for about three years. They were provided with a "conch" house on the beach. It was there, as the children swam and fished, that they had their first real introduction to tropical fruits and fish, all of which they were to encounter in the years to follow. At the time, there were no regular schools, so the children, again had to depend on their parents and the other adults in the community for their schooling. They both read voraciously, and to such an extent that when the time came for their next move, to Richmond, Virginia, young Erva was well ahead of her classmates in the language arts, but somewhat behind in mathematics. Brother Ralf was a whiz at everything he put his mind to, and was placed a grade ahead of his age mates.

From Virginia, their permanent move was to San Juan, Puerto Rico where Frank was assigned to be chief of the U.S. Weather Bureau, a position he was to hold for twenty-seven years. The children brushed up on their Spanish as this time they were headed straight for a school. Through their childhood years, both children learned to appreciate and respect the customs and culture of the people of Puerto Rico.

After graduating from high school, Erva went to normal school where she took a crash course in teacher education — she was to begin teaching "domestic science" in the fall at a school in

Bayamon. The trip from San Juan began with a ferry ride to Cataño followed by a train ride on a smoke-belching wood burner into Bayamon. She managed to get to the school in time to open up before the arrival of the students. Her task seemed impossible — the approved text was basic Fanny Farmer, but how does one use such a text in a place where most of the ingredients called for in the recipes were unavailable? The name of the game was "Improvise." If you can't get salmon, a nice fresh grouper will do. It was her hope that her students would be able to follow basic instructions, yet feel free to make additions or substitutions to create interesting meals that would also satisfy the local palate. In this, she did succeed.

In December of 1915, Erva was married to Paul A. Boulon, who was first-generation-French-born-in-the-USA from Long Island, New York. Knowing a good opportunity when he saw it, he started the first refrigeration business in Puerto Rico. Filling a very big need, the business flourished.

Between 1917 and 1923, four children, Erva Claire (better known as E.C.), Paul Jr. (Pablito), Ralf, and John (Jack) were born to the Boulons. By 1927, the business was keeping Paul Sr. so busy that the family decided that they simply had to have a summer place where they could escape the pressures of the job. They looked around Puerto Rico, but every place seemed too crowded, or too close to immediate civilization to suit their purposes. At about that time, Paul Sr. joined a fishing club with Denis Bay, St. John as its base of operations. It was on the return home from one of those fishing trips that he announced to the family that he had found "the spot." It was Trunk Bay.

The property was purchased in 1928, and Paul built a concrete cistern and warehouse on the beach. It was his plan to construct a "Great House" on the hill above the bay which would serve as the family's summer home. The warehouse would be needed not only for the storing of building materials, but also as a temporary shelter until the house on the hill was actually constructed. The plans for the building were drawn, and with the aid of a few friends, Paul precut and marked all of the lumber that was to be used to build the summer house. Then it was bundled and shipped on three sloops from Puerto Rico to Trunk Bay.

It was May of 1929, and the family was ready to make their first trip to St. John. Paul Sr. went ahead to meet the sloops as they arrived at Trunk Bay.

The *Catherine* arrived in St. Thomas at dawn on June the first after the overnight cruise from San Juan. The *Validor*, one of the three sloops, was in the harbor and was still laden with family's goods which meant that she had not yet been to St. John. Of course, the *Validor* was the one which carried some of the furnishings (the bedding), their baggage, and all of the comestibles they had packed up for their summer stay. It was not likely that their provisions would arrive in St. John for another day or two, as the captain was otherwise occupied with business in Charlotte Amalie.

Permission had been secured for the family to sail from Charlotte Amalie to St. John on the Navy fifty footer, and at 9:00 a.m. sharp, the sail got under way. It was a beautifully uneventful trip, except that one of the boys had a minor bout of seasickness. They landed in Cruz Bay at 11:00 a.m. and started the five mile walk to Trunk Bay.

In those days, the roads were trails which had been used by animal-drawn carts in Danish times, but most of them were now only just wide enough to accommodate people or animals walking in single file. Just after passing Caneel Bay, Mr. Francis, who said that he was heading for Cinnamon Bay, caught up to the Boulon parade and very kindly gave the boys a rest by letting them, in turn, ride his horse. The youngest, Jack, was six years old, and was lucky enough to travel most of the way on Mr. Francis's horse. Thank you's and goodbye's were exchanged at the entry trail to Trunk Bay, and the family proceeded to the concrete shed which had been built on the beach at the foot of the hill. (Today, only the cistern portion of that building remains).

Everyone was delighted with the sight before him. By this time, they were tired and hungry, but the beach was so beautiful, and the water so inviting, that the children stripped down to their underwear and ran down the beach into the water. Erva took her shoes off and soaked her feet in the bay while she mentally organized the rest of the day's meals. It was going to be difficult to prepare food, or to make sleeping arrangements with the *Validor* still in St. Thomas. Paul Sr. had the barest of furnishings and provisions, but it would suffice. At least there was water in the cistern, kerosene for the lanterns, and charcoal for the coalpot.

To their surprise and relief, the *Validor* arrived the following morning and the camping accommodations were made much more comfortable with the addition of the food, cots and mattresses. That first night had been quite cramped with six people on two mattresses which had been spread on some planks which had been placed on top of some oil drums. When they awoke, Jack was missing from the makeshift bed, and the first thought that crossed Erva's mind was that he had wandered down to the beach and.... To the relief of the family, he was found still fast asleep curled up in a little ball under the plank bed.

Paul Sr. stayed on for only two weeks. During that time, a trail was cut from the beach to the top of the hill, the foundation was laid out for the main house, and a lean-to kitchen was constructed on the beach, and; the Delco generator was installed which put the lanterns in storage and meant that they would be able to use the small refrigerator they had brought with them from Puerto Rico. Business matters were calling from San Juan and so Paul left with promises to return as soon as he could get away again. The family was really camping, but what a place for a campsite!

Erva had packed enough rice, dried beans and canned foods to last for the entire summer, but fresh vegetables, fruit and other perishables became an adventure to procure. There was no grocery just a short horse ride away, or a meat market to visit on Saturday mornings. There were plenty of fish in the sea and the children spent many hours fishing. The palm trees provided them with more coconuts than they could ever use, but oh, for some nice fresh produce.

Once settled, Erva and the children started taking regular walking trips around St. John - not only to meet the people and to see the island, but also to forage for anything fresh and edible. They always carried an Alpine basket and a small amount cash. Almost every family they met had chickens, and for a small amount of cash, Erva was able to get a few fresh eggs on each of her walking trips. Lots of bartering happened in those days, too. The family living at Cinnamon Bay had lime trees and raised pigs and other animals. In exchange for coconuts to feed the pigs, the family was given limes and a portion of the next slaughter. To this day the Boulons will affirm that no fresh pork tastes better than one which has been raised on coconuts.

On another trip which took Erva and the children to Susannaberg, Mr. Neptune Richards gave the family permission to pick fruit from his trees any time something was in season. It was a long walk from Trunk Bay, but the kind offer was gratefully accepted, and regular visits came to be a pleasant social event. From Mr. Richards they got soursops, sugarapples and mangoes.

Fresh vegetables often came in by sea. The commerce between the U.S. Virgin Islands and the British Virgin Islands was very active, especially trade with Tortola where ground provisions were grown quite plentifully. Learning that there was a family living at Trunk Bay, the captain of a Tortola sloop who was on his way to St. Thomas with fresh produce stopped in at Trunk Bay. Erva Boulon's delight at seeing fresh vegetables for the first time in more than a month was difficult to contain. The pot would have more than just rice and beans in it. From Tortola came raw brown sugar, breadfruit, sweet potatoes, cassava bread, tannias, plantains, bananas, sweet gourds, and large squashes, locally referred to as pumpkins. After the first transaction, the sloop captains made Trunk Bay a regular stop in their trade route during the summers when the family was in residence.

Wednesdays were set aside for trips to Cruz Bay. The mail was usually sorted by noon, and they were able to buy such basic staples as flour, cornmeal, salt, white sugar, cheese and few other groceries as well. At that time, it took most of a day just to get the things one needed for that day's meals. The pace was much slower because most people couldn't get anywhere faster than they could walk. The side benefit to this was that people really got to know each other. They took the time to say hello and to find out how the various family members "were keeping." It took a little time to buy a piece of cheese. It had to be cut from the wheel and weighed, and then it took a bit more time to do the calculation with pencil and paper that would result in the price. During the cutting of the cheese, one could find out that the grocer's sister had just had her third child. While the cheese was being weighed, the grocer might learn that your middle brother had gotten seasick on the sail over from St. Thomas. As the price was being figured, you might also learn that the mail wasn't ready because the boat was late in coming in this morning - they had been becalmed in Pillsbury Sound for two and a half hours.

The children grew strong and were happily a part of nature during their summers at Trunk Bay. During the second summer, the house on the hill was completed enough to be lived in and the furnishings could be left there in storage for the next visit. The family was there nearly every year until World War II broke out. The place was boarded up for the duration of the war and was not reopened until March of 1945.

By this time, Erva had been divorced for several years, and Paul Sr. was hospitalized with problems stemming from hardening of the arteries. He was to remain hospitalized until his death in 1953.

Times had been very lean for the family during the war years. Erva received no alimony or any of the family property after the divorce. A conference was held and it was decided that since the property on St. John was available for the use of any or all of the Boulon children, it seemed that the only logical thing to do was for Erva and her sons to return to St. John to see what could be done. The place was a terrible mess, but considering that no one had been there for six years, it wasn't that awful. The roof was still tight, but many of the shutters needed repairing and rebuilding. Once the house was cleaned and a fresh coat of paint was applied to the walls and woodwork, the place was quite presentable and comfortable.

The thought was to convert the old family home to an income producing venture - a guesthouse. Erva and Paul Jr. worked on the place together until May when a paying job came her way — that of managing Caneel Bay, which, prior to the war, had operated as a group of vacation cottages available for rent on a weekly or monthly basis. These buildings, too, had been shut down during the war years, and just as at Trunk Bay, much cleaning and rebuilding was necessary to make the place ready for paying guests. Erva continued to work at Caneel Bay until June of 1946.

The money which Erva earned at Caneel Bay went into the restoration and additional room construction at Trunk Bay. When they were ready to open for business, the main house had six rooms for rent. They had added a dining room and the roof area above it was made into a covered terrace which overlooked the bay. During 1946, John Anderson (author of *Night of the Silent Drums*), and his wife, Dean (also known as Adrienne Adams, the noted illustrator of children's books) stayed at Trunk Bay for several months. They became fast friends of the Boulon family, especially after having helped the Boulons with much of the work involved in the reconstruction of the place.

Trunk Bay operated as a guest house until 1958 when the property became a part of the Virgin Islands National Park. In January of that year, Erva Boulon married William Thorp who was building a guest cottage business at Little Maho. With Erva went the guest list and her wonderful recipes which had been developed over the years of running a guesthouse at Trunk Bay. She had, for years been faced with the problems inherent in feeding groups of people. The first food problem one encounters in the guesthouse business is how do to feed the typical tourist roast goat or grilled turtle steaks (turtles were plentiful then) in a way that will suit the American palate? Dinners were usually a surprise for everyone at the table. Once everyone agreed how wonderful everything was, that was when it was revealed, for example, that the fish was a moray eel and the "scallops" were from the wings of a sting ray. There were occasions when the beans got spilled ahead of time - like the time when a friend was invited to Trunk Bay for a roast goat dinner of which he was particularly fond. The routine was to have a cocktail or two before dinner on the terrace. The guests had a chance to relax before dinner, share stories of the day's adventures, and swap other pleasantries. The conversation invariably got around to speculations regarding what was going to be on the menu that evening.

"We had seagrape jelly with our breakfast, conch chowder with lunch, and sea urchins with our hors d'oeuvres. Wonder what the surprise is this evening?"

The extra invited guest then piped up with, "It's no secret. We're having one of the local kids for dinner."

When Trunk Bay was sold to the National Park, a small portion of the property was kept for the use of the family — Windswept.

This is now the home of the strawberry blond cyclist and marine biologist, otherwise known as Rafe Boulon. From a background of rugged individualists and survivors, he came. He was born in the Virgin Islands, and except for a few years in Puerto Rico during his early childhood, and another brief sojourn while studying marine biology, his life has been spent in the Virgin Islands.

At the entrance to the beach at Trunk Bay there is a sign proclaiming that the roadway is off limits to vehicles. Those who don't know, or who have not visited the Boulons in residence, are apt to become officious when Rafe, his family or guests ignore that sign and drive on to get to his house (built by Rafe and Kimberly themselves). That road is not for the faint of heart, and the drive from the house to the beach isn't just a major lesson in the concept of "down;" it's more like a crash course. The only other way to get into Windswept is by water and this route is not for the novice. The beach is fronted almost entirely by a barrier reef. By sea, there is one narrow channel in that treacherous stretch of reef upon which even snorkelers have run aground. Unless you know exactly where this slot in the reef is located, don't try it.

Rafe loves sailing and being with his kids. You can tell just how much he enjoys sailing when you see the expression on his face as he comes flying through that narrow slot in the reef at Windswept on his sailboard. He works with the children in the St. John K.A.T.S. (Kids and the Sea) Program every Saturday. The sailing team has won the Governor's Cup three times in a row, and his son, Devon, has been a member of two of those winning teams. Rafe has also been one of the stalwart dads in the steelband program. Devon plays, and Dad helps with the carting of the drums — the setups and take downs — for the majority of the band's performances. Rafe is a baseball widower. His wife, Kimberly, does the Little League duty in the family and is a hard working committee member for Young Athletes in Action. Both of the boys play ball, and between the two of them, they own over 6,000 baseball cards.

As a marine biologist, the part of the job Rafe loves best is field work - so much so that he has turned down promotions because they would take him away from nature and chain him to a desk.

As he puts it, he would rather count the rats on a small outlying cay than accept a promotion that would take him out of the actual sphere of study. He doesn't want to read and classify the reports of others - he wants to make the reports from his own observations.

"Why be a marine biologist if you're only going to get stuck indoors?" asks Rafe.

Would you really like to know something about turtles? Ask him. He'll tell you how you can become a part of the annual turtle watch. Are you concerned with the environment? Would you like to know what you can do to help? He'll tell you if you ask him. He won't preach, either. He'll tell you, in his calm, mild mannered way, some of the horrors he has observed and some of the things that each of us can do to prevent those horrors from happening again, provided that people will only take a moment or two each day for the sake of their world. Ask him about plastics. He'll tell you that there really is nothing wrong with plastics - just in how people use them and then dispose of them in a careless fashion. Plastic bags contribute to turtle starvation, and the plastic rings used to hold aluminum six-packs together have been found choking turtles and hobbling sea birds which have gotten them stuck around their necks and feet. He'll tell you. Just call the Division of Fish and Wildlife. You might even be able to arrange for him to take a class of children for a walk on the beach that will be both fun and educational.

Rafe's easy manner and ability to get along with people is a trait he inherited from the grand mistress of hospitality, his grandmother, Erva Boulon. Like her, he can immediately put his guests or new acquaintances at ease. He will do anything to avoid an unpleasant situation, figuring that life is too short to be tied up with useless confrontations. Don't make the mistake of thinking he's a doormat - he's been known to fight for what's right and fair.

To Kimberly, Rafe is husband and a core part of her life. To Devon and Revel, he is Daddy. To me, Rafe Boulon is favorite cousin — Erva Boulon was my grandmother, too.

Author Erva Denham says, "If World War Two hadn't happened, I'd have been born on St. John. Unfortunately, it did — and my family was temporarily called away from their home at Truck Bay, and I was born in Alameda California in 1946..."

Erva didn't stay away for long, however. She splashed ashore in Truck Bay from a seaplane at the age of two. She's been enthralled with the Virgins ever since. She attended grammar school in Cruz Bay (among her favorite teachers were Clarice Thomas, Roy Sewer and Melville Samuel), and she was the first St. John high school student to commute daily to St. Thomas (via the Caneel Bay ferry).

She currently lives on St. Thomas, and is at work on a novel about growing up on St. John.

Alan Smith
by
Amy Roberts

To look at Alan Smith, you'd never know he's a man on a mission. There's nothing about his contained demeanor, his calm precise speech, or his moderate behavior to suggest that inside of him burns an all-powerful spiritual force — and that this force is his primary motive for being on St. John, as well as everything else in his life.

Most people know Alan as the commissioner of the Department of Planning and Natural Resources during the late 80's, a position of power (second only to the governor, in some opinions) during those critical years of accelerated development. Others know him as a competent attorney whose side you definitely want to be on — whether the issue involves civil litigation, criminal or labor law.

Some people know Alan only by reputation, since he rarely hangs out on the streets of Cruz Bay. He and his wife Magda (the executive director of the VI Humanities Council) make a brief appearance at 6:59 a.m. as they hasten to the 7:00 ferry for their daily commute to St. Thomas. They stand out from among the other commuters only to those who are not used to seeing an interracial couple — a blonde German woman and a dark-skinned African-American man — looking professional and conservative, toting serious-looking briefcases.

But Alan and Magda have been an integral part of the island since they came to St. John to start a Baha'i community in 1976. Like all religions, the Baha'i faith is rich in complexity, but its philosophy can be summarized by three overriding beliefs: there is one God, all religions are one, and all of mankind is one human family. Its essential purpose is to eliminate prejudice — racial, religious, sexual — and create harmony and unity among people while celebrating their diversity and uniqueness.

"The prophet Baha'u'llah, the founder of the faith, says, 'The first and foremost method of teaching is deeds; let deeds, not words, be your adorning,'" said Alan. And so Alan and Magda, as well as 10 other Baha'is living on St. John, strive to become living examples of the ideals they hold. "Our faith has no clergy, so I have to share its teachings with the community, and defend it if it is attacked or questioned," he explained.

As part of their efforts, they have sponsored a series of evening workshops on racial harmony, workshops that successfully brought together the diverse elements of the community to open up to each other, to speak painful truths, and to begin to heal the wounds that racism has caused.

Because much as we might wish to deny it, racism *does* exist on St. John. Although the island may be paradise in a multitude of ways, it is not exempt from the turmoil that disturbs the rest of the world. Here on St. John, people of various colors and cultures "mix it up" much more than in most places. But when tension occurs in the community, the specter of racism rears its ugly head. Whether it's intended or not, a labor dispute, law enforcement situation, or act of rudeness is often interpreted as being racially motivated.

Perhaps that's to be expected on an island that was developed along strict color lines, with one group empowered and another enslaved. Although that era of oppression may seem like the distant past, it isn't, really; the plantation economy actually broke down much earlier on St. John, but slavery wasn't abolished in the Virgin Islands until 1848.

And certainly in the last 30 years, the island's population has gone through other radical changes, giving St. Johnians good reason to feel like a minority. Swelled by waves of white continentals from the United States, the population of permanent residents has easily quadrupled. More than a third of the island's residents now are white, according to the 1990 Census. Thirty years ago, only about 10% of the population was white.

Furthermore, in the Virgin Islands, racial distinctions are not made solely on the basis of color, but sometimes on whether one is "bahn heah" or not. One elementary teacher reported that only 20% of her students now were born to parents who were native St. Johnians; the vast majority are offspring of immigrants from other Eastern Caribbean islands. With this type of upheaval, it's no wonder that tensions exist.

Alan, however, remembers a more innocent time. "When we came in 1976, regardless of who you were, if you were interested in St. John, you were warmly accepted. But over time, this began to change for several reasons. As the economy changed, people came for reasons other than the love of the culture or the people. They came for economic gain and brought their prejudices with them."

He recalled the moment in the late 70's when he came aware of the change. "The Red and White Ball was an annual event that brought out the entire community. One night I went into town on the night of the ball and heard music playing at the Back Yard (bar). 'My God!' I thought. 'There are people who have established a separate lifestyle!' You could come here and no longer have to interact with the community. It's not an issue of race per se; it's often an issue of culture, and race is another layer."

Ultimately, Baha'is view the issue of race as illusionary. "Everybody is of one race that fanned out from East Central Africa," Alan explained. "We see differences of pigmentation as diversity with the race of *homo sapiens*. Culture, language, dress, food — these are further manifestations brought about by environmental conditions and changes. So race relations are meaningless — it's all human relationships, and how we learn to love and appreciate diversity. It's not easy. It's hard work."

Given the series of events and influences that make up Alan's past, it's not hard to imagine how he could have developed such a strong sensitivity to questions of race and culture.

Alan is the youngest of ten children who were brought up in Manistee, Michigan, a small, semi-rural town in the western part of the state. Although the Smiths were the only black family in the town itself (there were others in the vicinity), this never created an identity problem for Alan. "Quite clearly, I thought of myself as black. I never thought of myself as white," he said. "I grew up with white kids whom I loved." But he remembers disassociating himself from white friends who, naively intending no insult towards him, pointed to a group of black kids and said, "Look at those niggers!"

Alan was aware of the opportunities that Manistee offered, such as a year in Germany as an exchange student, that might not have been as available if he had been raised some other place. "Manistee had a good school system, and academic achievement was given a high priority in my family, despite the fact that my mother went to school only through the sixth grade, and my fathered died never learning how to read or write," Alan said. "But my father knew what he wanted for his children."

His father, Raymond Alexander Smith, now deceased, migrated from northern Florida to Michigan with his bride, Anna Mae, in 1929 to keep a job as a chauffeur when his employer moved. "My father was an excellent provider, and he did anything and everything to support the family," Alan said with obvious pride. "He carried coal, worked at an A&P, and was a self-taught cook. We had a family catering business for which we all worked. He was also an entertainer — a song and dance man — and he performed in hotels and was fairly well known.

"My father was a very loving man — that I never questioned — but he was also an angry man at times. That grew out of several factors," Alan explained. "He worked 18 hours a day. It was a constant frustration for him not knowing how to read or write, but he never had time to learn. His own father died when he was six, and he had to go to work then to help support a sister with polio, and so he struggled with his own sense of inferiority."

In spite of his lack of education, Raymond was a keen listener and observer who judged a person on the quality of his character, according to Alan. "Most of all, he was a man of uncompromised principles." Alan paused for a minute, shaking his head as he mused, "If I could live my life half in accordance with my own beliefs as my father did with his, I would have achieved something."

Alan said his mother's role in the household was typical of a black woman who headed up a large family. "She controlled everything but was almost unseen. She administered discipline and was deeply spiritual. She went though a lot when she moved with my father from the South to Michigan. When she recalls her first winter, she says she thought 'the whiteness of the snow would never go away.' That symbolizes a whole series of things she was grappling with as a young woman and mother." Anna Mae, now 83, still lives in Michigan where she remains active in community and church affairs. The family, "despite the internal squabbles and hurts that all families have," remains very close.

Alan views his family as "the classic Horatio Alger family." Indeed, Alan's own career seems to confirm that with one twist: "I don't say this with any pride, but I learned pretty early on that I could do whatever I wanted to do without much effort," he said. In 1965 he attended college at Michigan State, and four years later he enrolled in law school at the University of Michigan at Ann Arbor.

"Law school was, like, a drag," said Alan, briefly resurrecting the slang of the era. "I didn't enjoy the academics, so I treated school as a part-time activity," he admitted. Instead of giving a "stellar performance" as a student, he chose to get involved in radical politics and theater. Alan describes himself "as a good follower, but not a leader" in the Black Power Movement. "But I kept seeing people who were in the movement for their own personal advantage. They wanted power, and that disturbed me," he said.

In 1972 at the first meeting of the Black Law Students Alliance,

Alan became disenchanted with politics. "When I saw a guy who had passed out drunk on a bed one night get up the next day and give a 1965-style Stokely Carmichael speech and get elected, that confirmed for me that this wasn't about change; it was about power. And I really wanted change."

Alan, who had always had a thirst for the spiritual and a nature that led him to question the fundamentals, began to search for another solution to the problems he saw around him. During this time, he was involved in a protracted battle with the draft board over his imminent induction in the Army. Alan knew one thing: he was absolutely opposed to the war in Vietnam, and he was not going into the military.

"I chose to become a conscientious objector, which meant I had to write an essay based on religion on why I was opposed to war," said Alan. But he found it difficult to defend his position as a Christian who believed that "all men truly are brothers, when so many others who called themselves Christians had no problem picking up a weapon and killing each other."

In his search for a religious justification for his pacifism, Alan found that only one religion truly practiced "the oneness of mankind," and that was the Baha'i faith. "Baha'u'llah said all the prophets of God are manifestations of the Godhead; they are not incarnations of God. They come to every people throughout history.

"Over time, all religions run downhill, not because at the time they weren't manifestations of the truth, but because of all aspects of the created world. Everything in the created world has a cycle, and God has given man free will. Because of these two things, the teachings of the prophets — Moses, Jesus, Muhammad, the Buddha, Krishna — are perverted for the benefit of individual men. So to renew that force, God creates new manifestations."

Smith started to become seriously interested in this philosophy; however this was not his first encounter with the Baha'i faith.

"When I was 15, a minister came to our church who didn't give me a lot of pat answers and was willing to investigate the questions I asked. He took us on a field trip to Chicago, and as a side trip, we went to the Baha'i House of Worship. I was deeply moved and touched by the place, not by what anybody said, but by an aura, an ambiance, an ethos. A House of Worship has nine entrances, symbolizing the nine major world religions; the idea is you can enter the faith through any of these doors. I read the quotations from the writings of Baha'u'llah over each of these doors and was deeply moved."

During his college days, Alan met a number of Baha'is who impressed him with their intelligence, character, and spirituality, but it wasn't until law school when he met a woman through Legal Services that the big change came. "She was a bold, brassy, big black women, with unmatched 'native intelligence.' We became good friends. She was a staunch Christian who became a Baha'i. She looked me dead in the eye and said, 'Alan, there's always been one thing I've been able to do — recognize the truth.'"

"That made me think. I began to study religion. I went to the library and got books and read and meditated. I stopped going to classes and started attending Baha'i meetings, prepared to shoot holes in their ideas. But each time I left more convinced of the truth than when I went in. I said, 'Alan, this is the truth. You can turn your back to it, or you can commit to pursuing it.'"

His commitment took many forms, including the teaching of youth classes. One of his co-teachers was a German exchange student, Magda Guennewig. Alan recalled the first time he saw her at a meeting before he became a Baha'i. "I was seated on the piano bench opposite the front door, and in walked this woman in an aqua-green two piece outfit; I was immediately attracted."

Alan had an affinity for Germans, probably dating back to his own days as an exchange student. He soon asked Magda out, but the even was a disaster. "I was talking about Dylan, jazz, the Anti-Vietnam War Movement, and it was all going over her head. She understood the English, but it was a cultural problem. I left the date thinking, 'Hey, that's it!'" he said with a chuckle.

As they worked together, Alan and Magda began to discover their commonality. In 1974, they became engaged. Intermarriage is encouraged by the Baha'is as a means of bringing people together, but in order to marry, families must give their consent.

Difference in race were simply not an issue in Alan's family, but Alan and Magda were unsure about her father's reaction. They had a friend take a series of photos of Alan in different places, walking in the park, doing ordinary things. These were sent with a letter to her father asking for his blessing (her mother was no longer alive). He wrote back to Magda and said, "Your future husband looks like a kind man."

Some time after they were married, they took a trip to Germany which Alan described as "a wonderful experience. Germans are viewed as stand-offish, and German men are viewed as rigid. But I remember her father embracing me, with the tears flowing. It was a very warm feeling."

When they returned to the United States, however, Magda got a phone call saying that her father was in the hospital. "He died a week later, from a brain tumor. He never told anyone," Alan said quietly. "But," he said brightening, "I have a wonderful family in Germany."

Alan and Magda have one son, Derik, who graduated from the Antilles School in 1993. To Alan, "St. John has been an ideal place to raise a child of a mixed marriage because society is more accepting and responsive to it. Maybe this is due to the history of the island, and the Caribbean in general," he pondered. "Africans have not been in a minority position. Interracial marriages have not developed a taboo as they have in the States — a taboo that in only recent times is changing."

Derik decided to spend a year working at the Baha'i Center in Haifa before attending college. "Our emphasis has been to give Derik an identity as a Baha'i, rather than identify more strongly with a particular heritage. When Derik filled out college applications and reached the question about his race, he checked the box marked 'other.' When people are spiritually lost, they make an attempt to find themselves in the concept of Blackness, or Serbianess." This, Alan believes, inevitably leads to prejudice, war, and the dissension that is tearing the world apart.

"Human beings are at the apex of the physical world, but the nadir of the spiritual world," said Alan, "and things are getting worse." But that doesn't surprise him at all. "It's part of the process; we'll learn that as things become more violent, the only solution is a spiritual one. We're experiencing the death pangs, and the birth pangs, of a new order."

Although Alan sees the crack addict on the street as a tragic waste of human life, he also sees him as providing us with a service of a sort. "Every human being is part of the solution; those who are unconscious of it are in the process of destroying that which is no longer beneficial to mankind," he said philosophically.

"We are realizing that the world is falling apart, and society isn't coming up with the mechanisms to deal with it. I have a responsibility to reach out to one crack addict individually, but I can't reach out to all. And I can attach myself to the spirit of the time and a new spiritual order. When we recognize that our institutions are no longer working, we'll seek an alternative.

"Every individual must ask, 'What am I going to do about it?' Too few of us pose the question, and too few of us act," he stated matter-of-factly. "And the longer we deny it, the longer we suffer."

SOME TIPS FOR THE RICH AMERICANS COMING TO LIVE ON ST JOHN

by
Guy Benjamin

The most important thing to remember is that we are not savages still. If you take the time to find out, we are a nice and friendly people, who love other people. All kinds. We are respectful, having been taught from the cradle. We are polite, taking care never to hurt the other person's feelings, we are kind and loving, as all your younger non-maidens will attest.

We will not harm you or give you wrong information. We will never cheat you, and my friend Mrs. Fiona St. Clair will tell you of the time her daughter forgot her bag on the dock with all her valuables on her way back from Europe. She went halfway to Coral Bay, returned with all speed when she discovered it missing, and found it untouched, just where she had left it. That was a few years back, and no longer can I promise you such treatment, so do not expect it.

Once, in my glorious springtime, when I had to wait days for my check to become legal tender, I was on my weekend to St. Thomas. Milton arrived with my money from Cruz Bay. I had been promoted, and my salary was now $37.50 per month after nine years. My position was Principal Teacher. I couldn't wait. I had to ride a horse to Cruz Bay, catch the only boat leaving, and sail to St. Thomas. Do you know that boat would wait up to one hour for me! Henry or Wallace would pick me up on the other side. On this occasion, I forgot the envelope with the money on my desk in the Old Clinic where I lived. When I returned home on Sunday night, there on my desk was a folded note. "We had come to look for you. We closed up the house from the rain. Look in the bottom drawer for your money." John James, or St. Clare Lambert or Brooks. I don't know which. Just anyone. Don't you dare leave your house unlocked, unless it is by special arrangement with G.H.B. who is to return to "Catch a Jumbie." Twenty years later, or thereabouts, I had returned from my "sabbatical" with souvenirs, chains, gold pieces, and silver dollars. From a showcase in a locked house, they were all removed while I worked in St. Thomas.

Tip Number Six. Leave your house locked and your valuables in the refrigerator. That's the only place they won't look. Leave your German Shepherd inside. That's better. Why they won't look in the fridge? Easy. They don't like your cooking. It's not seasoned enough and tasteless besides. I can tell them better, but I won't. That's a promise. Not from the "Good Hands People." Only from me.

Tip Number One. For God's sake, say "Good morning," "Good day," "How do you do?" or "Goodnight" every time you see me. Don't worry I won't consider you are wanting to know me better, even if that is your ultimate reason. I'll say, "She has had good training," and since I don't know anything about the South, I won't blame it on training you received from a black mammy. I guess it also won't harm you (if you are elderly and respectful) to extend your hand to the minister, if you can recognize him. Some time back, he dressed in his black suit, and had a turned back collar. Today you may need to request credentials. Go to the church of your choice. It is a good place to go. Both the Moravians and Catholics shake hands in their communion services regularly. You'll get the feel of it and the black doesn't rub off! Now, please don't shake everyone's hand. Just some of us! The nice ones, like me, 'n Theovie, 'n Mother's Love. Us be gentlemens. Don't shake Fred han' or Milton's. Dem boys too bothersome, me son. Them ga' intentions. En don' shake Leroy own either. Him terrible. So very terrible dem gals does recommen he to dey frien' dem back home. When dey hit de warf, de fust name outter dey mouf is "Way Leroy?" All dem guys name Leroy. I hear's tell dat Charles 'n Rodney gettin' so populous too. Wonder if dem ever hear tell 'bout me? Anyone askin 'bout me, sen em strate to Crawl Bay roun' Bodo side. Lay em look at dey scenery.

Advice number seben. Sometimes I am really sorry that a number of you learned to write only one thing besides your name, "NO TRESPASSING." It seems as if written underneath and printed in red letters is the shouting message "For Whites Only." A better sign might read "Beware of the Dog." It is more humane than the "NO TRESPASSING" one. Today, when I see it on East End, I shudder. Guess many ances (plural of ants) scamper on my grave. Beautiful progress! We tore down my friend's house and put up the "NO TRESPASSING" sign on the poles. Guess that's for the Jumbies. "But they right there!"

Tip Number Three. Protect your privacy. You need not send us invitations to your parties. It is not expected. You may come to our Sunday School picnics, our fish fries and our funerals. We'll learn to recognize you. We may even invite you to our weddings. Then you have arrived! Guess you'll wonder why we refused to come to your cocktail party. No problem. High afternoon. Me son, I just getting home from fishing. Saturday at dat. She mussey crazy! En dem long frock she does be wearing to dem ting sitting down wid dem glass what look like pipe stem! En dem drink whar look purple like grape juice in sago when yo sick! Lard a messy! I'd get the ague, for sure if I drink any ob dem ting. Cocktail–Hentale! Ta la! Not for me, me son. Mary, you kin go if you want, but don't take de chilluns for God's sake. Neber!

Me? Neber me!

Tip Number Nine. Invite us if you want. We won't come. Curiosity won't kill a black cat. Besides, he ga nine lives anyhow...

Tip Number Fifteen. DON'T tip me everytime you come into Fred's and buy your favorite rum and coke or papaya daiquiri. You'll spoil me. I cannot report it on my income tax, so it goes to my favorite charity anyhow. A mister and his group had dinner the other day. He paid with sixty dollars in two notes. His bill totalled $53.00. I returned his change on a tray. He said, "Keep it." I didn't like the tone of his voice, so I left it on the tray. The group departed and left it there. Later, I picked it up and gave it to Fred. I couldn't even give it to charity. Poor Fred! That's not a fair comment. How could anyone know I am not an old bumbling waiter, down on my luck and glad for every tip? No comment. Instead, I'll tell you a tale.

I was at home on St. John during the past Easter vacation. I had gone to the Emmaus Moravian Church to practice on the organ there, since someone had borrowed (never to return) the speakers from the tone cabinet of my Hammond. On my way back, I must pass the Guy H. Benjamin Elementary School. A lady is taking a picture of the school and I stop, so as not to break up her camera. "Please come in and pose for me," she asked. "Certainly, on condition you'll send me a picture," I replied. "Done," she said. She took the picture and she requested my name and address. I had a package of mail on me, and I said to her, "Bet you aren't going to believe this," as I tore off the mailing label from a letter. She looked at the name, she looked at me, she looked at the school's name. She then looked again, in the opposite order. "No," she said, "but I still don't believe it." Then she put her worst fears into words. "You are telling me that this school is named after you?" "Yes," I replied quietly. A month later, I received the picture and a letter. She still doesn't believe it consciously. One day it might strike her as being really true.

Tip Number 99. DO BELIEVE EVERYTHING!

Tip Number Three or is it four? Learn to bargain. When you are in the market or store, don't pay exorbitant prices. You make it difficult for me. I can't live anymore. Better still, see how a native buys and what she pays. Then follow her example. We know you don't have to skimp. But we do! The name of the game is to learn from us as we do from you.

Tip Number Four and Five. As you hope to go to heaven when you die, these are most important. Somehow, they are mixed up with the "Thou Shalt Nots." Do not steal we husbands by being nice and seductive, or wily and charming, coiffed and textured, accommodating and different. Can't you see what that does to our ego, our pride, or "machocity" (a new ending only, not a new word)? That's fair also in war. But to take us away completely! Look at it this way. Who is to keep the home fires burning? After all, we are only men. Let's talk this thing over, reasonable-like. (Also, don't forget, that as long as you are on the Island, you will have a "name" for yourself, no matter what you may think to the contrary, and it is not a very respectful name).

Only one piece of advice left. Don't reread this chapter. Just let the natives read it. Remember to say, "Good morning and good night." We will not look at you the way we do in New York and shout through closed lips — "Wha' wrong wid 'e? He gan crazy? Wha he wan to t'ief? He t'ink he gun get in my house dat way? He too lie. Lay he keep he good marnin' for Venquelo en dem t'iefing Porto Ricans. I'm a native. Ah barn here. Ah no all de ropes. Lem me go ma way. He an he good marnin. Wha' i'lan he from? Marnin' indeed!"

Guy Benjamin of Coral Bay was the first St. Johnian to graduate from the Charlotte Amalie High School on St. Thomas. He has had a long, distinguished career as an educator. His book 'Me and My Beloved Virgin' is a Caribbean classic. The above story was reprinted from his second collection of stories about St. John which is entitled "More Tales from Me and My Beloved Virgin." He currently commutes between St. John and New York.

INDEX

Send orders to: American Paradise Publishing PO Box 37, St. John, VI 00831. Ph & Fax (809) 776-8346 or 693-8876.

Price List

	Cost
Sportfishing in the Virgin Islands...... "Everything You Need to Know!" by Carol Bareuther (120 pages, illustrated)	**$10.00 plus $2.00** S/H (ISBN 0-9631060-3-1)
Chasing the Horizon.................... "The Life and Times of a Modern Sea Gypsy" by Cap'n Fatty Goodlander (154 pages)	**$10.00 plus $2.00 S/H** (ISBN 0-9631060-1-5)
Seadogs, Clowns, and Gypsies............ "Twenty Modern Caribbean Sea Stories" by Cap'n Fatty Goodlander (65 pages)	**$7.00 plus $2.00 S/H** (ISBN 0-9631060-2-3)
Foxy and Jost Van Dyke................. "An Entertaining book on Foxy Callwood, the island of Jost, the Tamarind Bar, the Wooden Boat Race, and the JVD Preservation Society..." by Peter Farrell (120 pages)	**$10.00 plus $2.00 S/H** (ISBN 0-9631060-4-X)
St. John People......................... "Twenty Profiles of contemporary St. John residents written by a dozen St. John writers..." (235 pages, illustrated)	**$20.00 plus $3.00 S/H** (ISBN 0-9631060-5-8)
A Taste of the Virgin Islands........... "A delightful cookbook as rich and diverse as the multi-ethnic cuisine of the islands." by Carol Bareuther (155 pages, illustrated)	**Available Oct 93** (ISBN 0-9631060-6-6)
Exploring St. John..........by Pam Gaffin "A complete guidebook, with special sections on renting a car, hiking, snorkeling, and beach combing. (Illustrated, with numerous maps.)	**Available Nov 93** (ISBN 0-9631060-9-0)

Excerpt from **Seadogs, Clowns, and Gypsies** by Cap'n Fatty Goodlander...

It was like a scene from a picture postcard. An elderly couple — looking like they'd just fallen out from the pages of Modern Maturity magazine — strolled down a deserted beach on Jost Van Dyke in the British Virgin Islands. He wore the latest in yachting togs, she a simple floral dress. They held hands. The Trades rustled their silver hair. The caption on the back of the postcard might read, "The Golden Years — A Retired American Couple Vacation in Paradise."

They came upon a young West Indian fisherman dozing under a palm tree. They soon struck up a conversation.

The fisherman was relaxing after work, though it wasn't yet noon. He'd went out fishing, caught enough to feed his family, and returned to shore.

The tourists joked with him for being so lazy. "If you'd kept fishing, you might have caught enough fish to make it worth your time to bring them to St. Thomas and sell them to the restaurants," said the man. The tourist man had been in the wholesale meat business many years ago, and knew of such things. "Ya," said the fisherman, "dat true too, Mon."

"And if you'd fish a full day, five days a week, you'd probably soon have enough money to buy a real fishing boat with an inboard diesel engine, instead of having just an open outboard skiff..."

"Dat be nice," said the fisherman with a grin.

"With a real fishing boat, I'm sure you'd be able to increase your productivity," said the tourist. "If you were frugal, you'd soon have a little nest-egg set aside for another vessel..."

"Two boat fleet," said the fisherman excitedly, clearly getting off on the story. "But how I fish two boat when I only one mon?"

"You'd have to hire someone," said the tourist. "and with another man working for you — and you taking some of their profits — why in no time you could..."

"...retire, and lay 'round de beach all day in dey shade," finished the fisherman.

There was a long moment of silence, then the fisherman started laughing. He had a nice, clean laugh — totally without guile.

Then the tourist couple started laughing, and everyone was grinning at everyone else.

A bottle of unlabeled rum appeared, and they passed it around like kids. Even the woman bubbled the bottle.

They soon parted company, and each returned to their own world. The fisherman dozed off under the palm tree, and the tourist couple glanced at their gold Rolex watches — making sure they didn't miss the boat that would bring them to the plane that would return them to the rest of their lives...

Excerpt from **Chasing the Horizon** by Cap'n Fatty Goodlander...

I sailed into the Caribbean in the late '70s, a refugee from the 1960s. Like so many of my generation, I was restless, and driven, and disillusioned with America. I had loathed Chicago, Boston, and Miami — and felt like a Man Without a Country. While many of my friends 'returned to the farm', I sought a change in attitude through a change in latitude. The Lesser Antilles seemed a Sunny Place for Shady People. I fled southward.

The long passage was a rough one — a thousand ocean miles dead into the teeth of the Trades. I brought with me a rude boat carved by my own hand, a strong woman I wanted to share my life with — and not much else.

When we were finally able to ease sheets, we came roaring into Drake's Passage in the Virgins. The air was suddenly laced with the sweet, fruity scent of tropical flowers. The island of Tortola slid by to loo'ard — impossibly lush and green and mysterious. Coconut palms appeared to be waving welcome. Ripe papaya, mango, and breadfruit trees danced along the shores. Waves splashed diamonds on the beaches. Fields of bananas wiggled in the glinting sun.

Within that single moment of vivid memory —like a color slide plucked from a stack of black-and-white prints — I was forever smitten. The next few months of cruising confirmed it. My whole past life seemed mere preparation for my life as a Caribbean Sea Gypsy — with the immediate future as exciting as a tropical promise whispered by a sea shell. I suddenly wanted to kiss my existence full on the lips, without restraint nor care. My mid-latitude attitudes gradually shifted, and I was (once again) able to laugh like a child. For the first time as an adult — I was happy where I was.

Picture God's hands cupped into the most benign section of the Atlantic. A pool of fathomless blue, with His palms as South and Central America, and His fingertips as the Greater Antilles (Cuba, Hispaniola, Puerto Rico) and the Lesser Antilles — from the Virgins southward to Trinidad. Add the Nor'east Trade Winds — the mighty sun-kissed engine of it all. Color in the waters — from the clearest of whites to the palest of greens to the most eternal of deep, deep blues. Accept the jagged improbability of the jutting verdant islands of stone and rock and coral and tree — how lofty and solid and safe they squat upon the lapping sea.

Yes, I am hopelessly enthralled with the Caribbean.

She is a study in contrasts, this one million square mile mini-ocean; ever-changing yet always the same. Tranquil in her normal sleepy-eyed slumbers; she can become utterly savage in the blink of a hurricane's eye. She is noted for her peacefulness, and yet she is unmistakably untamed, wild, and primitive.

Her written history is one of idiocy. Cold white men in far-away places slashed at their treaties and contracts with mercilessly sharp pens — and the scuppers of their tropical sailing ships ran red with blood 4,000 miles away.

Cannons, sugar cane, and rum barrels soon dotted the shore. Pirates and missionaries and businessmen carved up the waterfront. Great cities were built even as their sponsoring empires crumbled. The harsh realities of the international marketplace rapidly showed all men — black, red, brown, and white — that the color of their blood, sweat, and tears were indistinguishable under a tropical sun.

Diversity? The Caribbean is as diverse as the peaceful Arawak Indians and fierce Caribe Indians of South America — as sophisticated as the ancient Mayans — as culturally rich as England, France, Spain, Portugal, Sweden, and Holland. Currently, the East Indian population on certain islands is growing nearly as fast as their West Indian. The growing live-aboard sailing community ("We're all here because we're not all there!") is primarily American — with a rich mix of European sailors drifting in from the east.

Throughout it all, of course, weaves the African. It is his culture — his music, his art, his dance — which permeates the Caribbean. His sun-washed smile, his elastic sense of time, his concept of family/tribe/community set the tone.

The poetry of Bob Marley, the literature of V.S. Naipal, the paintings of Haiti, those steel drums, that Calypsonian saying — are all fruits of the Caribbean Experience.

Luckily, the equatorial sun eventually bleaches out everything — even the stain of slavery.

People of Color are the majority in the majority of Caribbean Nations — and many of the most contented, most efficient, most prosperous islands are governed by a polyglot group of folks who have long ago ceased to care about the past political divisions or the bloodlines of their neighbor.

On certain of the smaller islands, boat builders are still more revered than lawyers; a fella who can catch fish is everybody's friend. A good outboard mechanic can become King — but would have to take a cut in pay.

Life isn't necessarily less complex — island society is quite sophisticated and subtle — but it usually *is* more in tune with its people. Harmony in the Caribbean isn't limited to church choirs. It is difficult to get angry when everything is OK, and has been for a long time, and probably always will be. There is no reason to rush. Tomorrow will be just as perfect.

By any measure, this mini-ocean is a wonderful place. But it is especially blessed for the cruising sailor — as if God, Walt Disney, and Joshua Slocum consulted to make a heaven on earth for sailors.

I'm still not jaded — despite the thousands of sea-miles we've sailed in the Caribbean over the last decade. Our charts are tattered, torn, and spider-webbed with faded courses. No matter. It is still fun. It is *still* a Sunny Place for Shady People...